T0365104

UNDERSTANDING THE COST OF POWER

SAMUEL ENEOJO ABAH

authorHOUSE®

AuthorHouse™
1663 Liberty Drive
Bloomington, IN 47403
www.authorhouse.com
Phone: 1-800-839-8640

All Scripture quotation are from King James Version of the Bible except otherwise stated

Published by AuthorHouse   04/13/2013

ISBN: 978-1-4772-2743-5 (sc)
ISBN: 978-1-4772-2744-2 (e)

ABOUT THE AUTHOR

Samuel Eneojo Abah is young man dedicated to the preaching of God's word with apostolic signs and wonders right from the age of 12. God in a notable revelation delivered to him a flourishing garden amidst desert. With this revelation came the mandate to restore mankind back to their lost glory through the ministry of reconciliation. He both believed and preaches the Word in its entirety.

He is the overseer of Samuel Eneojo Abah Ministries, an international, non-profit organisation committed to building responsible people in the society and in establishing holy people for God. He is a prophet and teacher of the word.

Sam is a First Class graduate of Microbiology. He does research in Molecular Biology of infectious diseases. He is married to Gloria and they are blessed with children.

ABOUT THE BOOK

This book will teach you how to experience and live in the full power of the Holy Spirit and the price you need to pay as nothing of value is free. It is what you need to live a triumphant lifestyle as a child of God. It reveals vital keys to accessing God's blessings and anointing in a mega dimension. It teaches you to be in command over your situation instead of your situation being in command over your life. The revelations in this book are the sure solution to your challenges. You can't read this book and not be empowered. Sit with it and read through. *For maximum impact, read it from cover to cover, never assume to be familiar with anything by mere looking at the caption. You have to read through because I am too sure you may have never taught of or encountered the revelations shared in this book.*

Welcome on board!

1

CONTENTS

DEDICATION

This book is dedicated to every child of God that desires to experience the presence and power of the Holy Spirit for greater exploits.

ACKNOWLEGEMENT

I acknowledge the HOLY SPIRIT for the strength and grace given to me to effectively communicate His will on the pages of this book.

I want to appreciate Gloria for her patience and endurance all through the period of writing this book; several times she has gone to bed alone while I work on this book and several times she will sit by me all night with the expression; 'you must succeed' on her face.

INTRODUCTION

Behold, I give unto you power to tread on serpents and scorpions, and over all the power of the enemy: and nothing shall by any means hurt you.

- Luke 10:19

You need power to rule your world. Do not live your life to fate. Be a determining factor for what happen around you and with you. You can choose what to allow into your studies, business, career, family, and ministry.

The existence of an enemy is real. An enemy is anything that hinders, opposes and stops your ideas, progress, and stable lifestyle.

The scripture above in the very words of Jesus confirmed that enemy exists and they posses power. They control and afflict their victims with their power. Their victims are those that are without power or little power or those that fail to recognise or use their God given power. Continuous affliction of the enemy over

5

your life is an indication that you are either powerless or you fail to use your power.

Christ gave us authority **over all** the power of the enemy because power (authority) is needed to control power.

When a strong man armed keepeth his palace, his goods are in peace: But when a stronger than he shall come upon him, and overcome him, he taketh from him all his armour wherein he trusted, and divideth his spoils

Luke 11:21-22

Your blessing is still lying in the hand of the devil because the devil is still stronger than you. satan has affected your mentality and you have been made to take your situation, science or doctor's report than the Word. You already believed that you can't have a good job because of your poor result, you already believed that you're not so beautiful to get married, you already believed that you are too old to get children and you already believed that the disease is incurable that is why your blessings are still kept in satan's custody. Until you

6

are empowered you cannot take what belongs to you. You need power to subdue and take all that the Lord has given unto you from satanic altars.

.... *through the greatness of thy power shall thine enemies submit themselves unto thee.*

Psalm 66:3

God has already given us the power (authority) over all the power of the enemy. This implies that God has delegated His right to command, determine and control to us. We have the audacity and the legal power to make and to enforce laws over the devil.

Nothing can harm us when we operate in full capacity of the given authority. We need to really behold (be conscious of) the power (authority) that has been given to us and use them, only then we can see the fall of satan in our daily lives.

Our number one enemy is the devil. He came to mankind in the Garden of Eden in the form of serpent and stole the blessings. The devil (satan) is the one responsible for the stagnation, failure, joblessness, marital delay, sicknesses and diseases in people's lives. A lot of people today say if God truly exist, why are there so many problems in the world? They get offset with God and they refused to believe in Him. They refused to understand that they are the ones that sold their privileges and right to the devil and they also rejects the power that God has given which is to be assessed through accepting Jesus as Lord and saviour. Unfortunately, not even all those that have accepted Jesus realize the use of this power that has been made available.

Jesus said He has given unto us His own power, meaning that he has delegated his authority to us, which implies that we can act exactly the way He would have acted and He will automatically approves any command that we give in His name.

The authority has to be in His name because it is a delegated authority and we are His representatives. Seventy of Jesus disciples returned and said, Lord EVEN THE DEVIL(S) were subject to us IN YOUR NAME

(Luke 10:17). They were surprised that even the devil(s) were subject to them when the used the name of Jesus. I could see the excitement on their faces, they were happy that they can do what their master has been doing.

The devil will always submit when you ditch out your authority in the name of Jesus.

Friends, you will always live and operate in the realm of Joy when you exercise the authority that Jesus has given you. Do not wait for God to come and deliver you, many today are complainers because they don't know how to use their authority. It is stupidity to be crying to God when you are supposed to give command; that was why John the Baptist was beheaded. Never think that crying to God is a sign of dependence on Him. You only depend on Him when you use the authority He has given you in his name.

I noticed that Jesus was seeing exactly the things that the disciple saw when they were commanding the devils: ***AND Jesus said to them, I beheld satan as lightening fall from heaven-Luke 10:18.***

In verse 17 they came saying the devils were subject unto us and in verse 18 Jesus said 'I was also seeing the devils falling like lightening from heaven' when you guys were commanding; this implies that Jesus was also listening to their command with automatic approval. That was why He was seeing what they saw. The delegated authority given to us by Jesus implies that He will establish whatever decree we make (Job 22:28) and sees what you see and says what you say.

What is that thing that is hurting you? Why keep asking if God exists? Let it be known unto you that you are the one holding yourself in that situation because I am too sure your release is now if you can effectively operate in the authority that Christ has given unto you.

No true child of God should be hurt. ***Nothing shall by any means hurt you.*** If your body or anything is hurting you right now, it is a sign that you need to be empowered by God.

Today, this power can only be delivered to us through the indwelling of the Holy Spirit. The power of the Holy

Spirit is the super power. It is the greatest power on earth, but the church is under utilizing this power.

Manifestation of the Holy Spirit power is not so common because people find it difficult to pay the price. Nothing of value is free. The manifestation of the Holy Spirit is in degrees (levels) and the full operation of His power is never without a price.

Every valuable thing is costly. There are prices you need to pay to be fully empowered by the Holy Spirit. Any kind of power has always been costly. The so-called power like Political power and satanic power are also not cheap, and those that need these powers pay the price for them. I remember hearing the story of a lady who was commanded to stay away from sex for so many years to obtain satanic power. People pay dearly to obtain witchcraft power. Some donate their children and they make this donation on a constant basis; *a woman once came to me confessing that she has killed more than 600 people in her witchcraft activities.*

There are a lot of evil sacrifices and satanic fasting and prayer today, just to receive power to destroy you and me (the church). Our power needs to exceed theirs to escape.

Have you not seen some religion declaring fasting and prayer throughout the world just to have power? Why do you think they are seeking for power? They seek for power to promote the kingdom of Satan and to oppress the people of God.

And when it was day, certain of the Jews banded together, and bound themselves under a curse, saying that they would neither eat nor drink till they had killed Paul.

- Acts 23:12.

Satanic agreement is real! Satanic covenant is real! Satanic dry fasting is real! You needs to wake up and lay hold on the original power to be able to cause destruction in the kingdom of darkness; else! You will perpetually remain under the bondage of satan.

You need to be empowered above the power of the enemy to posses your possession. You need to be engaged in biblical spiritual principles to enter into the kingdom of God; *a realm where no devil can oppress you, a realm where no devil exists*;

But if I with the finger of God cast out devils, no doubt the kingdom of God is come upon you.

-Luke 11:20

For us to enter into this realm we need to be empowered above the powers of the wicked and the hypocrites;

For I say unto you, That except your righteousness shall exceed the righteousness of the scribes and Pharisees, ye shall in no case enter into the kingdom of heaven.

-Mathew 5:20

We can only escape satanic affliction when our power supersedes that of the devils.

There are various dimension of the power of God and none of them are without prices.

In this book I will be showing the biblical principles that bring down power like fire and the prices you need to pay for them.

You are already on the right path to the solutions of your life as you read this book.

Welcome on board!

CHAPTER ONE

THE OUTPOURING OF GOD'S SPIRIT

And it shall come to pass afterward, that I will pour out my spirit upon all flesh; and your sons and your daughters shall prophesy, your old men shall dream dreams, your young men shall see visions: And also upon the servants and upon the handmaids in those days will I pour out my spirit.

-Joel 2:28-29

And it shall come to pass in the last days, saith God, I will pour out of my Spirit upon all flesh: and your sons and your daughters shall prophesy, and your young men shall see visions, and your old men shall dream dreams: And on my servants and on my handmaidens I will pour out in those days of my Spirit; and they shall prophesy:

-Acts 2:17-18

The Spirit of God is called the Holy Spirit. God promised that He would pour out the Holy Spirit upon us

15

'afterwards'. The word afterward implies the last days, considering the two scriptures above. When are the last days? The last days began right from the day the Holy Spirit came upon the disciples on the day of Pentecost because the word of God said the Holy Spirit would be poured out in the last days. If it weren't in the last days the Holy Spirit wouldn't have come on the disciples neither upon us today. We are and still in the last days.

The Old Testament is the dispensation of the father. The New Testament is the dispensation of the son, Jesus Christ and these last days is the dispensation of the Holy Spirit. That is why the Holy Spirit is continuously being poured out today.

To be ignorant of the Holy Spirit in this dispensation is to be ignorant of God. The Holy Spirit is the last seal to the church before the day of redemption.

And grieve not the Holy Spirit of God, whereby ye are sealed unto the day of redemption.

Ephesians 4:30

16

The promise is for all children of God without gender selection, race or status. The Holy Spirit is for men, women, servants and handmaids. It is also for those that the Lord will call (those that will be saved in the future);

For the promise is unto you, and to your children, and to all that are afar off, even as many as the Lord our God shall call.

-Acts 2:39

Your sons and daughters (your converts), servants and handmaids of God are those qualified to receive the outpouring of the Holy Spirit as clearly stated in Acts 2:17-18 and Joel 2:28-29. Note that the term *'all flesh'* in these scriptures does not mean all and sundry but anyone that can believe on Jesus irrespective of your gender, status or race.

The sons as daughters are those that believed on Jesus; *But as many as received him, to them gave He power to become the sons of God, even to them that believe on his name -John 1:12.*

17

The Evidence of the Baptism

The best evidence of the Holy Spirit baptism is the result of that baptism; just as the best evidence of a student performance in class is his result. It is the evidence of the Holy Spirit baptism that confirms the overwhelming presence of the Holy Spirit.

One of the evidence of the Holy Spirit is revelation. Sons, daughters, servants and handmaids shall prophecy; the young men shall see vision and the old men shall dream dreams. This is because dream needs experience to interpret. Prophecy, dreams and vision all has to do with revelation. Revelation is the most important thing in this last days and that is why the Holy Spirit is empowering people in that dimension. Revelation is one of the advantages that we have over the devil. The devil knows the scripture but he did not have access to the revelation that comes through the scripture.

The devil is the prince of this world;

The time for judging this world has come, when Satan, the ruler of this world, will be cast out

18

-John 12:31 (NLT)

Which none of the princes of this world knew: for had they known it, they would not have crucified the Lord of glory.

-1 Corinthians 2:8

If the devil had access to revelation, they wouldn't have crucified Jesus Christ because the death and resurrection of Jesus Christ is the worst thing that has happened to the kingdom of darkness.

This revelation is so important because of the diverse and strange doctrines and hypocrisy in these last days. How will we be able to identify them without revelation (2 Timothy 3:1-7).

Prophecy is a sure evidence of the Holy Spirit baptism. The ultimate form of prophecy is in witnessing Christ;

'for the testimony of Jesus is the spirit of prophecy.

Revelation 19:10

Everyone that is truly baptised in The Holy Spirit will be very thirsty to preach Christ.

The ultimate purpose of the Holy Spirit outpouring is to witness Christ;

But ye shall receive power, after that the Holy Ghost is come upon you: and ye shall be witnesses unto me both in Jerusalem, and in all Judaea, and in Samaria, and unto the uttermost part of the earth

- Acts 1:8

The Holy Spirit is meant to testify of Jesus; to reveal the truth about Jesus to people.

But when the Comforter is come, whom I will send unto you from the Father, even the Spirit of truth, which proceedeth from the Father, he shall testify of me:

-John 15:26

Speaking in tongue is the initial evidence of the Holy Spirit. Anyone that is baptised in the Holy Spirit will speak in tongue as evidence.

And they were all filled with the Holy Ghost, and began to speak with other tongues, as the Spirit gave them utterance.

-Acts 2:4

This speaking in tongue is not to be manipulated; it is as the Spirit will give you utterance. It is very advantageous to pray in tongue. You confuse the devil each time you speak in tongues. If the devil did not know your request he cannot stop the answer to your prayers as he did to that of Daniel (Daniel 10:13).

For he that speaketh in an unknown tongue speaketh not unto men, but unto God: for no man understandeth him; howbeit in the spirit he speaketh mysteries.

-1 Corinthians 14:2

Speaking in tongues is speaking in the Spirit because it is the language of the Spirit. It is the mystery of the Holy

21

Spirit given to you in prayer for effective communication.

Despite the fact that the apostles have the promise of the Holy Spirit, they have to wait and pray in the upper room to receive this power. Promises of God are delivered on the altar of prayer. You need to tell God that you need it before you can have it.

And when the day of Pentecost was fully come, they were all with one accord in one place. And suddenly there came a sound from heaven as of a rushing mighty wind, and it filled all the house where they were sitting. And there appeared unto them cloven tongues like as of fire, and it sat upon each of them. And they were all filled with the Holy Ghost, and began to speak with other tongues, as the Spirit gave them utterance.

–Acts 2:1-4

Can you see the kind of prayer that brought down the Holy Spirit? They deliberately left their houses and refuse to return. They remain until the day of Pentecost was fully come. What were they doing? Prayer of course! They were praying in agreement (one accord) for the Lord Jesus to send down the promised power. Why don't they choose to just claim and wait for the promises of God? Friends! It is true that God has promised you but I am afraid you will wait for it till eternity except you wait on God in prayers.

We need the Holy Spirit before we can effectively bind and loose. This is because the Holy Spirit is the link between earth and heaven. He is the person that establishes in heaven the decrees that we make on earth because He both bears record on earth and in heaven.

For there are three that bear record in heaven, the Father, the Word, and the Holy Ghost: and these three are one. And there are three that bear witness in earth, the Spirit, and the water, and the blood: and these three agree in one.

-1John 5:7-8

Verily I say unto you, whatsoever ye shall bind on earth shall be bound in heaven: and whatsoever ye shall loose on earth shall be loosed in heaven.

                                    -Mathew 18:18

The Holy Spirit establishes the decrees we make on earth in heaven, without Him one cannot know the mind of God in heaven, neither would our prayer finds relevance in heaven:

Likewise the Spirit also helpeth our infirmities: for we know not what we should pray for as we ought: but the Spirit itself maketh intercession for us with groanings which cannot be uttered.

                                    -Roman 8:26

The Holy Spirit prays through us. Now you can see that the dimension of your prayers will change if you are baptised in the Holy Spirit. So many hardly know what to pray for but when the Holy Spirit comes on you it makes intercession through you with groaning that cannot be uttered. This implies the deepest form of prayer, it is beyond utterance: It is called speaking in an unknown tongue. When a power plant is generating power it makes groaning (heavy noise), when an aeroplane is about to take off it makes so much noise because certain amount of power/energy is needed to overcome the force of gravity. The groaning dimension of prayer generates power (energy of God) in us and is what we need to overcome.

As humans we have so much infirmity (flaws) that we hardly know what to pray for. Many times we ask to consume it upon our lust (James 4:3). Again, our knowledge is limited but the Holy Spirit is unlimited, He knows our past, present and future. Only with Him we can pray effectively.

The kingdom of God is all about the power and the person of the Holy Spirit.

I believed you understand by now that the Holy Spirit is a person and when we talked about being baptised in the Holy Spirit we meant being heavily possessed by Him. Many are familiar with being possessed of the devil with witchcraft spirit, water demons and such like but few are familiar with the baptism or being heavily possessed by The Holy Spirit. It is amazing that many that doubts the existence of God never doubts the existence of the devil and evil spirits like the spirit of witchcraft but that is by the way.

My emphasis here is that the Holy Spirit is a person and has always been personified in the Bible;

Howbeit when he, the Spirit of truth, is come, he will guide you into all truth: for he shall not speak of himself; but whatsoever he shall hear, that shall he speak: and he will shew you things to come.

-John 16:13

He is a person, He can come (move), guide, speak, hear and show which means He got legs, have senses, mouth, ears and hands. He can also teach, meaning that he have intellects;

But the Comforter, which is the Holy Ghost, whom the Father will send in my name, he shall teach you all things, and bring all things to your remembrance, whatsoever I have said unto you.

-John 14:26

Not only that he can teach but he is also a comforter (advocate, helper, and councillor). Your life will be helpless, comfortless and totally messed-up without Him. He can teach you all things and bring all things to your remembrance.

Recall that the disciple forgot many things that the Lord had told them before His death because they were yet to be baptized with the Holy Spirit. They forgot that Jesus said he would resurrect on the third day.

And they entered in, and found not the body of the Lord Jesus. And it came to pass, as they were much perplexed thereabout, behold, two men stood by them in shining garments: And as they were afraid, and bowed down their faces to the earth, they said unto them, Why seek ye the living among the dead? He is not here, but is risen: remember how he spake unto you when he was yet in Galilee, Saying, The Son of man must be delivered into the hands of sinful men, and be crucified, and the third day rise again. **And they remembered his words,**

-Luke 24:3-8. Bolden, mine

When therefore he was risen from the dead, **his disciples remembered that he had said this unto them;** *and they believed the scripture, and the word which Jesus had said.*

- John 2:22

These things understood not his disciples *at the first: but when Jesus was glorified,* **then remembered they** *that these things were written of him, and that they had done these things unto him.*

- John 12:16. Bolden, mine

The disciples were always suffering from misunderstanding and forgetfulness. To misunderstand or forget the word of God is to live a life of misery.

The Holy Spirit is the person that always stood with us to teach and remind us the word of God. He is a person!

28

Your life will change when you recognise the Holy Spirit as a person.

I remembered the encounter I had on the 10th of December, 2012 while preparing for my usual bible teaching and fire service. I was praying on my knees and I suddenly saw in a vision a personality behind me dressed in white extraordinary indescribable suit, His appearance was like a cloud (shadow like but bright shadow not dark as usual). He walked up to me and asked, where will you want me to sit and I replied, front seat of course! He then said stand up from your knee and prepare for your meeting because it is 5 minutes past 8 and when I stood up from my knees and checked the time it was so.- Guess who this personality is!-THE HOLY SPIRIT. I then dressed up for fellowship. That night amazing wonder happened. Short sightedness, broken bones and all sort of healing took place. A woman evangelist that came for the meeting all the way from Kent, UK could not touch me because of the anointing. There was a strong flux (the Holy Spirit electric force field) around me that she cannot penetrate. She made several attempt to touch me but she would hardly come before she fell under anointing. Power will always surge within you anytime you recognize that the Holy Spirit is living inside you as a person.

CHAPTER TWO

THE HOLY SPIRIT AND POWER

But ye shall receive power, after that the Holy Ghost is come upon you: and ye shall be witnesses unto me both in Jerusalem, and in all Judaea, and in Samaria, and unto the uttermost part of the earth.

- Acts 1:8

The baptism of the Holy Spirit does not automatically translate into the baptism of power or anointing. You may probably at this time have gotten the Holy Spirit or may have seen people in your local assembly that claimed to have the Holy Spirit baptism as evidenced in speaking in tongues. But do all with the baptism of the Holy Spirit generate the same power? No of course!

'But ye shall receive power, after that the Holy Ghost is come upon you'. The power comes after the Holy Spirit is come upon you meaning that the Holy Spirit is the link to the power of God. It is the conveyor of the power of God.

31

It is one thing to be baptised in the Holy Spirit and another thing to be baptised into power (anointing) by the Holy Spirit. It is this power dimension of the Holy Spirit that is called the anointing.

How God anointed Jesus of Nazareth with the Holy Ghost and with power: who went about doing good, and healing all that were oppressed of the devil; for God was with him.

-Acts 10:38

Here again you can see the distinction *'with the Holy Ghost and with power'*. Anyone that is truly baptised in the Holy Spirit has all what it takes to be empowered but this is not automatic. That is why I am talking about the cost of power. There are certain things you need to do to access the power that come through the Holy Spirit.

The Holy Spirit baptism is like the generator: If you want the generator to produce power you have to make a conscious effort to kick-start the generator

'How God anointed Jesus of Nazareth with the Holy Ghost and with power'. It is both the presence of the Holy Spirit and the power of the Holy Spirit that is called the anointing. You can have the baptism of the Holy Spirit without fully experiencing the anointing but you cannot have the anointing without the baptism or presence (as in the Old Testament) of the Holy Spirit.

There are times the baptism of the Holy Spirit will come with its entire power in full operation like what happened on the Pentecost day. But! Remember that the apostles were *wet with prayers* before that happened. They left their houses and were gathered waiting just for the Holy Spirit for several days. They left their occupation and declared private holiday just to wait for the Holy Spirit in prayer. They resolved their differences and united together in one accord, they were in awesome fellowship with the same mind and the same goal before the power package of the Holy Spirit came with the baptism. You can receive the power (anointing) with the baptism if you seek it this way.

That is the cost of power!

33

In summary, you will need the Holy Spirit before you can be empowered. The Holy Spirit is the ultimate and most potent source of Power.

Remember that the kingdom of God is not in words but in power.

But I will come to you shortly, if the Lord will, and will know, not the speech of them, which are puffed up, but the power. **For the kingdom of God is not in word, but in power.**

– 1 Corinthians 4:19-20

Paul said the kingdom of God is not in talking but in Power. The kingdom of God will have no meaning in the world without power. Jesus was not only mighty in words alone but also in deeds:

And he said unto them, what things? And they said unto him, concerning **Jesus of Nazareth, which was a prophet mighty in deed and word before God and all the people:**

-Luke 24:19

The power is what produces the deeds! The devil did not fear your grammar or your oratory power, He only fears and bows to the power of God. The power of God in us gives us victory over the kingdom of darkness and over all the works of the devil.

Behold, I give unto you power to tread on serpents and scorpions, and over all the power of the enemy: and nothing shall by any means hurt you.

-Luke 10:19

The power of God in you places you *above all devils*. You can only be oppressed if you are powerless, which is why many are so weak and sickly. The power of God at work in you is meant to silent the devil. **Oppressors only submit to higher power;**

Say unto God, How terrible art thou in thy works! Through the greatness of thy power shall thine enemies submit themselves unto thee.

-Psalm 66:3

35

The Holy Spirit power is the ultimate power because He is the Spirit of God and He is God.

Everything about God is holy. His word is called the Holy Scripture, His kingdom is holy, His Spirit is holy and likewise He expects His people to be holy. ***The power of the Holy Spirit dwells only in Holy Vessels.***

It is unfortunate that the power of God is dying out of many Christian organisations today and that is why so many churches are dying and some folding up. Some churches today are mere using oratory power but the real power of God is lacking.

A lot of us goes to church today not because we see the power of God but because of tradition and culture, "my father was a Catholic, Anglican, Pentecostal etc., that is our church" sort of. There are so many church leaders today without power. They have the desire to serve God but the power is not there and if the power is not there the result will not be there and because the results are not there, they begin to struggle and many start looking of alternatives contrary to the will of God. You need power

36

to back up your desire to serve God irrespective of any service you are rendering to God.

You do not need to be a pastor to have the power of God. Business men and women also need the power of God, Students need the power of God, professionals need the power of God, your family need the power of God, fathers, mothers and yourself need the power of God. You will begin to see changes in your life, career, business, studies, and ministry when you are operating with the power of God.

God commissioned me to write this book to awaken the children of God all over the world so that they can begin to operate in full capacity. God is about to begin with you.

Power can only come when we seek for it;

Ask, and it shall be given you; seek, and ye shall find; knock, and it shall be opened unto you:

-Mathew 7:7

If ye then, being evil, know how to give good gifts unto your children: how much more shall your heavenly Father give the Holy Spirit to them that ask him?

-Luke 11:13

The Holy Spirit is a good gift but this gift is given to them that ask. Not mere seeking but being desperate, seeking it with all your heart;

But if from thence thou shalt seek the LORD thy God, thou shalt find him, if thou seek him with all thy heart and with all thy soul.

-Deuteronomy 4:29.

The seeking that guarantees answer is seeking with the whole of your heart, it is seeking Him above job, money, above all others.

So many people goes about today with tittles without power. There are no entitlement in tittles, what you need is power. God want us to have power.

Let every soul be subject unto the higher powers. For there is no power but of God...

- Romans 13:1.

No power is recognised when the power of God is in operation.

When a strong man armed keepeth his palace, his goods are in peace: But when a stronger than he shall come upon him, and overcome him, he taketh from him all his armour wherein he trusted, and divideth his spoils.

-Luke 11:21-22

You need the power to overcome and to take what belongs to you.

The Holy Spirit is the true source of power. All other powers are not power before Him. It is the power in form of a person that is given to you and me to deliver us from the strong man of affliction, it is the power that will teach us the things of God and helps us to live the life of holiness.

But the Comforter, which is the Holy Ghost, whom the Father will send in my name, he shall teach you all things, and bring all things to your remembrance, whatsoever I have said unto you.

-John 14:26

But the anointing which ye have received of him abideth in you, and ye need not that any man teach you: but as the same anointing teacheth you of all things, and is truth, and is no lie, and even as it hath taught you, ye shall abide in him.

-1John 2:27

The Holy Spirit is the Spirit of God and is God. The Spirit of God is the power of God. There is no power than of God. It is not said to be power unless it is from God, at most it could be considered as powerless power. The power of God is above all other forms of power because it is from above; *For I know that the LORD is great, and that our Lord is above all gods.*

-Psalm 135:5

He that cometh from above is above all: he that is of the earth is earthly, and speaketh of the earth: he that cometh from heaven is above all

-John 3:31.

The power of God is above that of magicians and sorcerers, it is above the power of witches and wizards, and it is above cultism. It is a supernatural power that can swallow the magic of the devil against your life;

And Moses and Aaron went in unto Pharaoh, and they did so as the LORD had commanded: and Aaron cast down his rod before Pharaoh, and before his servants, and it became a serpent. Then Pharaoh also called the wise men and the sorcerers: now the magicians of Egypt, they also did in like manner with their enchantments. For they cast down every man his rod, and they became serpents: but Aaron's rod swallowed up their rods.

- Exodus 7:10-12

The power of the Holy Spirit is the swallowing super power.

And the magicians did so with their enchantments to bring forth lice, but they could not: so there were lice upon man, and upon beast. Then the magicians said unto Pharaoh, This is the finger of God: and Pharaoh's heart was hardened, and he hearkened not unto them; as the LORD had said.

-Exodus 8:18-19

It is the power that specialises in doing what man cannot do. Impossibility is the area of specialty of His power. Right now I see the power working impossibility into possibility your life in Jesus name. I see this power changing and shaping your world. It is the 'making power' and I declare that this power will 'make you' in Jesus name.

The Holy Spirit is the power that makes the word of God to have impact on the people, it is the power that can draw customers to your business, it is the power that can make you succeed, it is the power that can deliver you

42

from serving and being subject to satanic dictates, this power guarantees your freedom from ancestral power, bad dreams, sexual contaminations in the physical and in the dream, it is the power that can make notorious sinner to submit to God, It is indeed the original power and all other power bows to it.

A lot of people are subject to fake powers because the power of God is absent.

The people of Samaria had for a long time been subject to fake power demonstrated by Simon the sorcerer because the power of God was not present. They are so many people like Simon in our days using fake power to control people's lives.

The only way you can expose the powers of wickedness is to be empowered by the Holy Spirit. The power of God is what truly disgrace and expose fake powers. When the power of God shows every other power will submit.

Then Philip went down to the city of Samaria, and preached Christ unto them And the people with one accord gave heed unto those things which Philip spake, hearing and seeing the miracles which he did. For unclean spirits, crying with loud voice, came out of many that were possessed with them: and many taken with palsies, and that were lame, were healed. And there was great joy in that city. But there was a certain man, called Simon, which before time in the same city used sorcery, and bewitched the people of Samaria, giving out that himself was some great one: To whom they all gave heed, from the least to the greatest, saying, This man is the great power of God. And to him they had regard, because that of long time he had bewitched them with sorceries. But when they believed Philip preaching the things concerning the kingdom of God, and the name of Jesus Christ, they were baptized, both men and women. Then Simon himself believed also: and when he was baptized, he continued with Philip, and wondered, beholding the miracles and signs, which were done. Now when the apostles which were at Jerusalem heard that Samaria had received the word of God, they sent unto them Peter and John: Who, when they were come down, prayed for them, that they might receive the Holy Ghost: (For as yet he was fallen upon none of them: only they were baptized in the name of the Lord Jesus.) Then laid they their hands on them, and they received the Holy Ghost. And when Simon saw that through laying on of the apostles' hands the Holy Ghost was given, he offered them money, Saying, Give me also this power, that on whomsoever I lay hands, he may receive the Holy Ghost. But Peter said unto him, Thy money perish with thee, because thou hast thought that the gift of God may be purchased with money. Thou hast neither part nor lot in this matter: for thy heart is not right in the sight of God.

-Acts 8:5-21

Can you imagine a whole town under the influence of the spirit of sorcery and witchcraft operating in Simon? This is what is called territorial powers! The scripture above said both the poor (least) and the greatest (rich) were subject to his witchcraft. It is indeed a fact that territorial demons exist. Deliverance came to them in Samaria when they believed the gospel of Philip. There

45

will be no hope of being delivered until we believed the gospel because in the gospel of Christ is power.

Everyone needs the gospel irrespective of your status in the society. The gospel is the power of God. The Holy Spirit moves through the word of God (the gospel).

For I am not ashamed of this good news about Christ. It is the power of God at work, saving everyone who believes—the Jew first and also the Gentile.

-Roman 1:16 (NLT)

How dare you be ashamed of the gospel? Why are you ashamed of being known as a child of God? That must be satanic deception. Stay openly identified! It is foolishness to be shameful of what is gainful. Why are you ashamed of salvation? That must indeed be caused by the devil who never wants anyone free. There is a saving power in the word of God and until you believe you cannot be saved. The word of God is not meant to produce shame, it is meant to generate power. The power of God is at work in every word of God that proceeded out of God. The word of God is full of power and that is why we can live (have a successful life) by it;

'Man shall not live by bread alone, but by every word that proceedeth out of the mouth of God

- Mathew 4:4.

So many today thought that they can only live by money (bread), and they pursue it and forget fellowship with God. When you pursue money, you may get only what the money can give and not what God can give. Our life indeed cannot be complete without the word of God.

> **The power of the Holy Spirit is the solution to every situation of your life and not money....This power is not only for ministers of the gospel it is also for the fulfilment of your destiny**

There are things that money cannot do for you. There are diseases that are incurable by money only by the power of God.

The power of God cannot be bought with money else; it will be too difficult for some man to purchase it. The only price is prayer, sacrifice, faith and labouring in the word of God.

Simon had taught that he could buy the power of the Holy Spirit with money. He realized that the power supersede money so he tried to be smart by offering money for it. Not knowing that the power cannot be bought with money. You cannot use your money to deceive God or men of God.

There are many things that money cannot do for you; the power of the Holy Spirit is the solution to every situation of your life, not money. When you have the power of God money will be the by-product.

There are many people like Simon who has extreme desire for power but do not know how to get it. Simon the sorcerer believed and was baptized in water during the ministry of Philip. He was astonished at the dimensions of power at work in Philip but he did not have access to this power. He suddenly discovered that the power he had previously was a powerless power; the power in your pocket, body or home has long been confirmed as a powerless power and that is why you must do away with them.

Though Simon believed and was baptised in the name of Jesus (water baptism), yet his heart was not right with God and that was why he did not know the right approach to access divine power. His heart was not sanctified and until ones heart is sanctified one cannot access the power of God.

> **Until ones heart is sanctified one cannot access the power of God.**

The place of sanctification

Sanctification is the second work of grace after salvation. It leads to the transformation of your heart and set you aside for the master use. It is the removal of the Adam's nature. It is different and definite from salvation.

The outcome of sanctification is the lifestyle of holiness.

Salvation is the forgiveness of your sins, which leads to justification as though you have never sinned. Note that at salvation it was the confessed sins that were forgiven i.e. all the sins you have committed until now (the time of confession). Salvation is what makes old things (lifestyle) to pass away. Salvation gives you the opportunity to begin a new life. Salvation makes you a new creature because as far as God is concerned you are a new person and all your sins have been buried;

This means that anyone who belongs to Christ has become a new person. The old life is gone; a new life has begun!

-2 Corinthians 5:17(NLT)

It is the old life that is forgotten giving you the opportunity for a new life. But there is possibility of falling back into sin; *My little children, these things write I unto you, that ye sin not. And if any man sin, we have an advocate with the Father, Jesus Christ the righteous:*

-1John 2:1

Here the scripture talked about little children (the born again). Note that one of the attributes of little children is misbehaviour. They were instructed not to sin but if they sin they will have an advocate with Jesus. But one needs to seek the help of an advocate (confession) to get it. You still remain justified only if you confess and seek the help of the advocate who is Jesus Christ.

When falling into sin and confession becomes frequent the feeling of frustration will set into your Christian journey. Some may fall away while others will begin to think it's impossible to live a holy life.

> **Sanctification is what actually prevents you from continuous rising and falling as a child of God.**

But how long will one continue to rise and fall in sin?

Sanctification is what actually prevents you from continuous rising and falling as a child of God. It helps you to maintain a daily walk with God in fear and reference.

Salvation is what guarantees the forgiveness of your sins while sanctification is what guarantees your freedom from sin.

At sanctification, the root of sin is removed. It is a higher level of growth after salvation when an inner urge of sin is completely cut off; it is the level of gaining command over besetting sin making you able to live like Jesus Christ;

Be ye therefore perfect, even as your Father, which is in heaven, is perfect.

-Matthew 5:48

If perfection is unattainable Jesus will not say that we should be perfect. Sanctification produces the lifestyle of holiness (perfection) because the root of sin has been removed. The preservation of your Christian race is not guaranteed until you are sanctified. Sanctification preserves your body, soul and spirit blameless; it is a wholesome experience. It preserves your salvation unto the coming of our lord Jesus Christ;

And the very God of peace sanctify you wholly; and I pray God your whole spirit and soul and body be preserved blameless unto the coming of our Lord Jesus Christ.

- 1Theselonians 5:23

When you got born again it is your spirit that got born again but the body is not yet free and that is why some are still under generational family curse, which comes according to the flesh. The body is always hungry to commit sin. *That which is born of the flesh is flesh; and that which is born of the Spirit is spirit.*

- John 3:6

So you can see that being born of the Spirit (note the capital letter 'S' meaning the Spirit of God) means that the Spirit of God redeems your spirit, which is different from being born of the flesh. The flesh's desire is sin. It is only with the help of the Spirit (the Word) that we can

53

conquer the flesh. The Word conquers the flesh through its sanctifying power. I will not like to be too detailed here as some of these things are explained in my book titled, *Now that you are born again.*

We need to posses our vessel i.e. our body in sanctification;

That every one of you should know how to possess his vessel in sanctification and honour;

- 1 Thessalonians 4:4.

And the very God of peace sanctify you wholly; and I pray God your whole spirit and soul and body be preserved blameless unto the coming of our Lord Jesus Christ.

-1Theselonians 5:23

Note the phrases 'sanctify you wholly', 'whole spirit, soul and body', and the word preserved. We are sanctified wholly and then preserved blameless unto the coming of the Lord Jesus Christ. What is preservation, it is keeping back from spoilage, from corruption and decay. The WORD said we are sanctified wholly (spirit, body and soul) and preserved blameless. There is no place in the Bible that says we are sanctified in part or partly (gradually) sanctified. Those explanations are philosophies of men. It may take some time to experience the blessing of sanctification but it is attainable.

Sanctification is a wholesome experience and not what you experience in part. If you got the ability to live above telling lies you can also have the ability to live above fornication if those abilities are produced by the power in Word of God, except if you are trying with your own power.

They is no point of one being sanctified from fornication while one still fall to the sin of lying occasionally, it then means that you are yet to be preserved (sanctified) in readiness to the coming of the Lord. The finished work of grace is done once and for all.

So Christ was once offered to bear the sins of many; and unto them that look for him shall he appear the second time without sin unto salvation.

-Hebrew 9:28

Understand that Christ was offered once both for the world and for the church. The offering of His life for the world is to purchase our salvation from sin.

For God so loved the world, that he gave his only begotten Son, that whosoever believeth in him should not perish, but have everlasting life.

-John 3:16

The offering of His life for the church is to sanctify and cleanse it to become glorious without spot or wrinkle or anything that defiles;

Husbands, love your wives, **even as Christ also loved the church, and gave himself for it; That he might sanctify and cleanse it with the washing of water by the word, That he might present it to himself a glorious church, not having spot, or wrinkle, or any such thing; but that it should be holy and without blemish.**

-Ephesians 5:25-27

This implies that after your salvation you become a member of the body of Christ (The church), after which you need to press for the second work of grace, which is sanctification.

The same provision was made once for both of them, which is Christ's death on the cross.

'That he might sanctify and cleanse it with the washing of water by the word, That he might present it to himself a glorious church, not having spot, or wrinkle, or any such thing; but that it should be holy and without blemish'.

We can see here again that we can be sanctified by the Word and that the purpose of sanctification is to present the church a glorious church. The church is you and I. Sanctification removes spots and wrinkles (you may call it besetting sin) from us. It makes us holy without blemish, which is why I said earlier that it is the removal of Adam's nature (the root of sin).

Let me give you an illustration; Salvation is like saving or redeeming a man that has fallen into the pit and sanctification is like washing him up from the dirt and putting on him a new garment, removing the old garment that has been soaked in the mud.

Sanctification really means 'set apart' for the master's use. God will not use anything that is defile or partly holy. He may call you in your unworthiness but He will always qualify you to use you. He takes the imperfect and perfects them.

God uses holy vessels. His word is not partly holy, His Spirit is not partly holy and His kingdom is not partly holy. God operate with the principle of complete holiness and obedience.

If a man therefore purges himself from these, he shall be a vessel unto honour, sanctified, and meet for the master's use, and prepared unto every good work.

-2Timothy 2:21

Sanctification is indeed the work of grace that we experience after salvation that enables the church (you and I that are born again) to live a sinless life.

> **Christ offered his body not only for the sin of the world but also for the sanctification of the church**

Christ offered his body not only for the sin of the world but also for the sanctification of the church; the children of God (the born again). He gave himself to the church to purify and sanctify it.

Note that both God and man have parts to play in sanctification;

And the very God of peace sanctify you wholly; and I pray God your whole spirit and soul and body be preserved blameless unto the coming of our Lord Jesus Christ.

-1Thessalonians 5:23

Here we see that God sanctifies to preserve us blameless unto the coming of our Lord Jesus.

Let me show you the part you need to play;

For I am the LORD your God: ye shall therefore sanctify yourselves, and ye shall be holy; for I am holy: neither shall ye defile yourselves with any manner of creeping thing that creepeth upon the earth.

-Leviticus 11:44

And Joshua said unto the people, sanctify yourselves: for tomorrow the LORD will do wonders among you.

-Joshua 3:5

Note that these people are already the people of God but God still call them to sanctification. Sanctification is what makes us live a holy life. The similitude of what God was saying here in the Old Testament is what Apostle Peter said to the strangers scattered throughout Pontus, Galatia, Cappadocia, Asia, and Bithynia (1 peter 1:1);

But as he which hath called you is holy, so be ye holy in all manner of conversation; Because it is written, Be ye holy; for I am holy.

- 1 Peter 1:15-16

So you can see that there is a part you need to play; you need to constantly pray to remain in the Spirit. I have noticed in my own life that sin become impossible anytime I am fully operating in the realm of the Spirit.

This I say then, Walk in the Spirit, and ye shall not fulfil the lust of the flesh.

Galatians 5:16

Those that live in the Spirit thinks it is impossible to become carnal and the carnal feels it is impossible to be holy and many today belong to this carnal group of people thereby saying that it is impossible to live a holy life in this world. They usually quote Roman 3:23 but they did not read the verse before and after and they also fail to recognise that that was the description of the original state of man.

Sanctification is real and those that have attained it know what I am talking about;

When I was born again I usually fall in to sin of lying and I will weep and confess, another day it will happen again until I was tired. I then began to pray for sanctification and now I noticed that I don't lie anymore; now lying smells!

Simon could not access the power of God because His heart was not sanctified and when ones heart is not sanctified his approach will always be wrong because his thoughts are still defiled. *"For as he thinketh in his heart so is he (proverb 23:7)"*.

Again, notice that the bible recorded that Simon's heart was not right with God.

Thou hast neither part nor lot in this matter: for thy heart is not right in the sight of God.

Acts 8:21

But remember that he has been believed the gospel and have been baptized. Yet his heart was not rise with God because his heart has not been sanctified. The root of bitterness is still springing up in him. He fell from the grace of God.

Looking diligently lest any man fail of the grace of God; lest any root of bitterness springing up trouble you, and thereby many be defiled;

- Hebrews 12:15

The experience of Simon should teach us that salvation from sin at confession alone is not enough. We need to press forward (Philippians 3:14). I suppose that if Simon had died in the state of his heart then he would have probably missed heaven;

Who shall ascend into the hill of the LORD? or who shall stand in his holy place? He that hath clean hands, and a pure heart; who hath not lifted up his soul unto vanity, nor sworn deceitfully.

-Psalms 24:3-4

But recall that Simon's heart was not right with God (Acts 8:21). But we thank God that Simon realized and pleaded for mercy. (Acts 8:24).

They are many people just like Simon that believed but do not know how to access the power of God, most of them derailed looking for alternatives. Some of them move from assembly to assembly, from church to church, from men of God to men of God for laying on of hands.

Power do not just come so cheaply, anointing is not cheap, anointing comes from accumulation of much prayer, studying the word of God and engaging in

> **Anointing comes from accumulation of much prayer, studying the word of God and engaging in spiritual biblical forces for power**

spiritual biblical forces for power and not just by mere laying on of hands.

You may say that Moses laid his hand on Joshua but remember that Joshua has been involved in the ministry of Moses:

And Moses said unto Joshua, Choose us out men, and go out, fight with Amalek: tomorrow I will stand on the top of the hill with the rod of God in mine hand.

-Exodus 17:9

God himself recognised the consecration of Joshua. Joshua was a faithful consistent and obedient servant of God and Moses.

And the LORD said unto Moses, Take thee Joshua the son of Nun, a man in whom is the spirit, and lay thine hand upon him; And Moses did as the LORD commanded him: and he took Joshua, and set him before Eleazar the priest, and before all the congregation: And he laid his hands upon him, and gave him a charge, as the LORD commanded by the hand of Moses.

-Numbers 27:18, 22-23

And Joshua the son of Nun was full of the spirit of wisdom; for Moses had laid his hands upon him: and the children of Israel hearkened unto him, and did as the LORD commanded Moses.

-Deuteronomy 34:9

Joshua has the spirit of God but was full of it (the spirit of wisdom) that is being empowered when Moses laid his hand upon him. The power of God can be imparted to heal your body through laying on of hands but for the anointing (full operation) as in the case of Joshua, God and his servant will have to see your devotion and consecration. I lay hand on people to pray for their healing but not for the intention of transferring the anointing of God on me except if you are a ready/willing vessel. Power is not cheap!

Do you really understand the depth of what Elisha did to gain power? We will further discuss this later in this book. But understand that anointing is not cheap. You got to wait on the Holy Spirit to be empowered.

The right place to access power

And, behold, I send the promise of my Father upon you: but tarry ye in the city of Jerusalem, until ye be endued with power from on high.

-Luke 24:49

And when the day of Pentecost was fully come, they were all with one accord in one place. And suddenly there came a sound from heaven as of a rushing mighty wind, and it filled all the house where they were sitting. And there appeared unto them cloven tongues like as of fire, and it sat upon each of them. And they were all filled with the Holy Ghost, and began to speak with other tongues, as the Spirit gave them utterance

.-Acts 2:1-4

The right place to access power is in the upper room (on your prayer alter). Jesus told his disciple not to rush into ministry but to tarry (wait persistently) in the city of Jerusalem, until they are endued with power from above.

They gathered together and raised an alter of prayer, they wait patiently for the promised power and suddenly the power of God came upon them.

The description of this power interests me: *a rushing mighty wind and filled where they were sitting. It appears like cloven tongues of fire.* The Holy Spirit came rushing because the prayer was so intense that heaven cannot withstands it. The power descended carrying fire with it and the fire resembling tongues sat upon them meaning that their tongue was transformed with the power of God and the evidence was that they spake in new tongues.

The power of the Holy Spirit is likened to fire;

I indeed baptize you with water unto repentance: but he that cometh after me is mightier than I, whose shoes I am not worthy to bear: **he shall baptize you with the Holy Ghost, and with fire (power):**

Mathew 3:1. In bracket mine

You are only ready for power encounter when you begin to call upon God to empower you; there is no other alternative. The Holy Spirit remains the only and effective source of power. God is ready to mightily pour His power upon you if you are ready.

What is this power for?

Most assembly today are filled with people speaking in tongue but lacks the demonstration of the power of God. The church of God is not evangelising anymore, we left the devil and his agents to be preaching their own message to us when we are supposed to be preaching the gospel of salvation to them.

> **What is the anointing of Holy Spirit meant for? Is it for 'speaking in tongue' alone the? We speak so much tongue as evidence that we are filled with the Holy Spirit and there are no power demonstration, no evangelism!**

What is the anointing of the Holy Spirit meant for? Is it for speaking in tongue alone? We speak so much tongue as evidence that we are filled with the Holy Spirit and there are no power demonstration, no evangelism! People that claim to be filled with the Holy Spirit are running away for the devil, they are always on the defensive side while Satan and his agents are on the offensive side. When are you going to torment the kingdom of Satan and let them be on the defensive side rather than you?

By the grace of God I am translated from being on the defensive side to the offensive side. Satan knows that I am born to torment the kingdom of darkness and this I do always because I have been empowered by God and I consistently recognise my place in Christ Jesus stirring up the Spirit that is in me.

I went to my hometown for a church project that God instructed me to do. While at home, a sister came and told me that one of my childhood friends is seriously vexed with the spirit of insanity. I asked her to be brought to my house and they did. I kept her in the visitor's room and prayed for her and immediately she regained her sanity back. She was the third person that got delivered from the spirit of insanity while on holiday in my hometown. The other guy's insanity was about 10 years. He was bound with chains and then locked up at home. The mother came and said man of God, come heal my son, I told her go and you will meet your son seated in his right mind. Truly, she left and met her son seated in his right mind. The chains on him broke on its own accord as no one has access to that place let alone breaking the chains. The sister was surprised as his son greeted her in his right mind. It was this unusual form of greeting that drew her attention to go near her son when she suddenly discovered with amazement that the chains were broken. Hallelujah! Today God will break every chain that is holding you in bondage in Jesus name. You don't wait for the devil to first attacks you; be the first to attack him and you will notice he will flee away from you.

A woman came to me confessing that she had killed more than six hundred (600) people including her relations and neighbours by giving them food in the dream. The woman confessed that people she feed in the dream usually die within a month and her major centre of operation are in churches, I asked her to tell me the name of those churches and I was surprised that she was mentioning the so called popular churches that we have in that country. She came confessing because I ministered in their church the previous day and I declared war on all the powers of witches and wizards in that vicinity. She was seriously tormented and came confessing. Praise God! Be the first to declare war. Are you ready? I now declare fire on anything that has kept you from progressing in Jesus name. Receive your job, receive your children, receive your glorious marriage, receive journey mercies, receive your freedom from ancestral power, and receive your prosperity in the mighty name of Jesus.

If you are empowered demons will not mess up around you. Do not wait to be attacked to keep on defending yourself all the time. You should attack the kingdom of darkness too. Jesus is a tormenter of the devil. They know Him.

And, behold, they cried out, saying, what have we to do with thee, Jesus, thou Son of God? Art thou come hither to torment us before the time?

-Matthew 8:29

You should be a tormenter of the devil if the same Spirit that is in Jesus is in you. When will you stop running for the devil? You need power!

I was hosting a prayer meeting in the northern part of Nigeria with one of my partner who testified of a woman that got healed from the spirit of insanity in his ministry. The testimony was amazing and it really stirred us up. I stood and challenged the people, asking them if the power of the Holy Spirit is for speaking in tongue alone. I

**If you are empowered demons will not mess up around you......
You should be a tormenter of the devil if the same Spirit that is in Jesus is in you.**

immediately stood up and I also declared to my partner (in demonstration of power too) that God is going to give him a man-child 'him that pisseth against the wall' because at this time he desired to have a man-child. I told him that his wife will conceive and in nine months time she will be delivered of a boy and it happened exactly as I said. That was power in demonstration!

God wants believers to demonstrate power over the works of the enemy but today we come together only to defend ourselves from demons and pray protective prayer. God knows that I have for long stopped praying protective sympathetic prayer. I pray prayer of authority. Jesus wants you to have authority over the devil and authority to preach the gospel, and that was the commission He gave us after His resurrection.

And he said unto them, Go ye into all the world, and preach the gospel to every creature. He that believeth and is baptized shall be saved; but he that believeth not shall be damned. And these signs shall follow them that believe; In my name shall they cast out devils; they shall speak with new tongues; They shall take up

73

serpents; and if they drink any deadly thing, it shall not hurt them; they shall lay hands on the sick, and they shall recover. So then after the Lord had spoken unto them, he was received up into heaven, and sat on the right hand of God And they went forth, and preached everywhere, the Lord working with them, and confirming the word with signs following. Amen

- Mark 16:15-20

Can you see the dimension of power that God has given you? This power is something that you need to exploit. You cannot use this power if you do not realise and know that it is meant for you. Don't be ignorant of the power of God, tap into it and exploit it. It is time for you to demonstrate the power of God. If you got it, you cannot hide it.

> **You cannot use this power if you do not realise and know that it is meant for you....if you got it you cannot hide it.**

CHAPTER THREE

EXPLOITS THROUGH POWER

Please understand that the Holy Spirit was in God's team in the creation of the world. *He is the catalyst of all creation. Man may make things but God create things. Things that are made are made up of things that have been created.* That is why I pity those scientists, professionals and anyone that says there is no God.

The fool hath said in his heart, there is no God. Corrupt are they, and have done abominable iniquity: there is none that doeth good.

- Psalms 53:1

I am the LORD, and there is none else, there is no God beside me: I girded thee, though thou hast not known me:

- Isaiah 45:5

It is foolishness for anyone to think that there is no God. Some claim that God did not create them that they just evolved. Evolved from what? Assuming atoms and molecules comes

> **The Holy Spirit is the catalyst of all creation. Man may make things but God create things. Things that are made are made up of things that have been created.**

together, who would have created those atoms and molecules? In July 4, 2012, the world announced the existence of Higgs boson-like particles on BBC and they

> **Evolved from what? Assuming atoms and molecules comes together, who would have created those atoms and molecules?**

claim to have gotten the fundamental understanding of the universe (though not fully proved) using a large hadrons collider, a particle accelerator. Where are the sources of that photon? Who made them? How do they come to exist? Well! I am not trying to prove the existence of God to you, as I will not like to do the work of the Holy Spirit. You got to believe God by faith but I will like you to understand that God the father, God the son (Jesus) and God the Holy Spirit created you and the universe.

In the beginning God created the heaven and the earth. And the earth was without form, and void; and darkness was upon the face of the deep. And the Spirit of God moved upon the face of the waters. And God said, Let there be light: and there was light.

–Genesis 1:1-3

And God said, Let us make man in our image, after our likeness: and let them have dominion over the fish of the sea, and over the fowl of the air, and over the cattle, and over all the earth, and over every creeping thing that creepeth upon the earth.

-Genesis 1:26

The darkness in your life is not an issue if the power of the Holy Spirit is available. God created the earth and the earth was without form but the Holy Spirit was moving upon the face of the deep (earth) and God said let there be light and there was light. The role of the Holy Spirit was to catalyse into action the words of God. The Holy Spirit moved on the face of the water incubating the words of God into maturity thereby bringing shape to the world and pushing darkness aside.

The Holy Spirit must incubate words before they can be delivered. ***The move of the Holy Spirit is what gives birth to the demonstration of power.*** Can you see that even God has to ensure that the Holy Spirit moved before He spoke? The move of the Holy Spirit is very important because it gives your words power. Power in words is not in quotable quotes or semantic similarity between words as has filled the pulpit of our days.

God is looking for those He will place His hand upon because God can only send man to man. Even when he send an angel they have to come in the form of man; this has been a principle with God. He sends his son Jesus in

> God is looking for those He will place His hand upon because God can only send man to man.

the form of a man. God does nothing on earth without a man. He needs men to send and to anoint. Everyone that truly demonstrates the power of God in the Bible or in this contemporary time did so by the empowerment of the Holy Spirit.

Enoch

And Enoch walked with God after he begat Methuselah three hundred years, and begat sons and daughters:

-Genesis 5:22

Enoch demonstrated the power of holiness. You need power to walk with God in these evil days. I announce to you that walking with God is in itself a dimension of power demonstration. Enoch walked with God for 300 years, this seems unimaginable to the carnal mind! He was neither ahead of God nor behind God. He

> In this our day holiness is no more a common Christian virtue anymore because we lack the power of the Holy Spirit.

79

remained in perpetual holiness with God for 300 years.

In this our day holiness is no more a common Christian virtue anymore because we lack the power of the Holy Spirit. Sin cannot near you if you are charged by the power of the Holy Spirit. Anyone that enjoys fellowship with God will keep away sin.

Praying in the Holy Ghost has immensely helped me to live above sin. I know I have to be on my prayer alter morning, afternoon and evening and I do enjoy my fellowship with the Holy Spirit, so I know how bad I am going to feel if I dare commit sin.

Whosoever is born of God doth not commit sin; for his seed remaineth in him: and he cannot sin, because he is born of God.

-1John 3:9

There is a power in us to make us resist sin. Enoch operated in this power. This power is called the seed (Word) of God.

Thy word have I hid in mine heart, that I might not sin against thee -Psalms 119:11

Enoch has showed it to us that the life of holiness is possible. If it was possible to him in the old covenant it is also possible to us in the new covenant.

What happened to Enoch when he walked with God?

By faith Enoch was translated that he should not see death; and was not found, because God had translated him: for before his translation he had this testimony, that he pleased God.

-Hebrew 11:5

I have told you earlier that working with God is a demonstration of His power. There is a translating power in walking with God.

And he saith unto them, Follow me, and I will make you....

-Mathew 4:19

Follow Christ if you want to be made, those that follow Him will always experience one form of translation of the other. God will make you the person you want to be if you follow him. You need faith to follow God. You need to trust Him that He can change your situation if you leave your illegal business else you cannot follow Him.

Enoch built and demonstrated faith in God while walking with God. He demonstrated power over death. He was translated instead of dying. Those that follow God cannot see corruption.

.......Thou shalt not suffer thine Holy One to see corruption.

-Acts 13:35

Enoch was a man that obtained testimony of being pleasing to God. Which testimony have you gotten in this your lifetime? Which power have you demonstrated? I want you to understand that it was the empowerment of the Spirit that enables Enoch to walk with God. It was the Spirit of God that translated him.

82

His translation was a demonstration of the power of the Holy Spirit.

You can be so empowered that your body will be translated by the Spirit of God; translated from sickness to health, oppression and depression to absolute peace. These will be your portions in Jesus name.

Joshua

And the LORD said unto Moses, Take thee Joshua the son of Nun, a man in whom is the spirit, and lay thine hand upon him; And Moses did as the LORD commanded him: and he took Joshua, and set him before Eleazar the priest, and before all the congregation: And he laid his hands upon him, and gave him a charge, as the LORD commanded by the hand of Moses.

-Numbers 27:18, 22-23

And Joshua the son of Nun was full of the spirit of wisdom; for Moses had laid his hands upon him: and the children of Israel hearkened unto him, and did as the LORD commanded Moses.

-Deuteronomy 34:9

Joshua was a man filled with the Holy Spirit; he was filled with the Spirit of wisdom. The children of Israel listened to him because of power of God that is working in him. If you have the power of God people will obey you, they will be submissive to you. Even the kingdom of darkness will be submissive to you.

...through the greatness of thy power shall thine enemies submit themselves unto thee.

-Psalm 66:3

The power that is at work in Joshua is the power of possession and dominion and that is why he went on conquering and conquering.

Now after the death of Moses the servant of the LORD it came to pass, that the LORD spake unto Joshua the son of Nun, Moses' minister, saying, Moses my servant is dead; now therefore arise, go over this Jordan, thou, and all this people, unto the land which I do give to them, even to the children of Israel. Every place that the sole of your foot shall tread upon, that have I given unto you, as I said unto Moses From the wilderness and this Lebanon even unto the great river, the river Euphrates, all the land of the Hittites, and unto the great sea toward the going down of the sun, shall be your coast. There shall not any man be able to stand before thee all the days of thy life: as I was with Moses, so I will be with thee: I will not fail thee, nor forsake thee.

-Joshua 1:1-5

Possession is a proof of power. Powerful people will posses and conquer the land for Jesus. With power also comes support. Joshua was one of the Judges of Israel that got the absolute support of the people.

Whosoever he be that doth rebel against thy commandment, and will not hearken unto thy words in all that thou commandest him, he shall be put to death: only be strong and of a good courage.

-Joshua 1:18

Jericho that was strictly shut up because of the children of Israel fell not with bows and arrow or artillery and bombs but with the power and the Spirit of wisdom at work in Joshua. God gave him the strategy. The Spirit of God is a strategist; if you walk with Him you must succeed. The strategy of God is the best. God's way is the

> **The Spirit of God is a strategist, if you walk with Him you must succeed.**

best way. Threat lives issues God's way; fight your battles God's way, get your money God's way, run your family/business God's way and do the work of God God's way. God's idea is the best idea. God's idea is what is needed to bring down that wall of Jericho in your life.

So the people shouted when the priests blew with the trumpets: and it came to pass, when the people heard the sound of the trumpet, and the people shouted with a great shout, that the wall fell down flat, so that the people went up into the city, every man straight before him, and they took the city.

-Joshua 6:20

This kind of shout is not an ordinary shout; it is a shout of power. They blew the trumpet and what comes out was power. I see every wall hindering your access to your inheritance shattered in Jesus name.

Gideon

And there came an angel of the LORD, and sat under an oak which was in Ophrah, that pertained unto Joash the Abiezrite: and his son Gideon threshed wheat by the winepress, to hide it from the Midianites. And the angel of the LORD appeared unto him, and said unto him, The LORD is with thee, thou mighty man of valour. And Gideon said unto him, Oh my Lord, if the LORD be with us, why then is all this befallen us? and where be all his miracles which our fathers told us of, saying, Did not the LORD bring us up from Egypt? but now the LORD hath forsaken us, and delivered us into the hands of the Midianites. And the LORD looked upon him, and said, Go in this thy might, and thou shalt save Israel from the hand of the Midianites: have not I sent thee?

-Judges 6:11-14

But the Spirit of the LORD came upon Gideon, and he blew a trumpet; and Abiezer was gathered after him. And he sent messengers throughout all Manasseh; who also was gathered after him: and he sent messengers unto Asher, and unto Zebulun, and unto Naphtali; and they came up to meet

-Judges 6:34-35

Every times people cry unto the Lord He will always raise a deliverer to save them but what if no one is ready? I want you to realise that power will not come if there is no burden in your heart. Gideon was full of burden in his heart because of what they were passing

88

> **Do you know that the way God sees you is different from the way men see you? Men focus at what you have acquired but God focuses on the potentials within you.**

through in the hand of the Midianites. The angel of the God appeared unto Gideon while at work and said to him "you mighty man of valour". He was surprised at the salutation; he did not expect it at all. Do you know that the way God sees you is different from the way men see you? Men focus at what you have acquired but God focuses on the potentials within you.

Gideon's assignment wouldn't have been possible without the Spirit of the LORD. The Spirit of God is the force behind every exploit in God's kingdom.

Gideon was able to accomplish this great task of deliverance because of the Spirit of God. Gideon was clothed with the Spirit of God and he blew the trumpet and the Abiezer were gathered together in support of him, that same trumpet that he blew quickly raised messengers to the Manasseh, Asher, Zebulum and

Napthali and they were all gathered together unto him. Again, we could see the power in anointed trumpet. People blew the trumpet under the leadership of Joshua and the wall of Jericho fell, Gideon blew the trumpet and people gathered, Jesus said let there be light and there was light. All these are made possible by the power of the Holy Spirit.

Go and seek for power on your knees and the dark powers militating against your ministry will disappear. Your business is almost empty because you lack power, all other shops are selling but yours is dry without customers. You accuse them of using evil powers but why don't you use the power of God too. You need power to activate whatever God has given to you, you need power to fulfil your destiny else you will become a shadow of what God created you to be.

Gideon's accomplishments in securing deliverance for his people in pulling down the evil alter are power driven. No power, no exploit!

Elijah

You are supposed to be in command as a child of God. Being a child of God makes you a solution. *I was in an airbus (Lufthansa) flying from Frankfurt to Nigeria when the person in front of me collapsed, this guy was immediately fainting, the air hostesses gathered but they know not what to do, I sat directly at the back of this man and I was watching all that was going on. I did not initially want to say anything but the Holy Spirit ministered to me saying, Samuel my son you are a solution and I will like you to lay your hand on this guy. I then asked the guy, would you like me to pray for you? And he replied yes. I then say a very simple prayer in Jesus name. He was instantly healed and went to the toilet himself; this was the guy that could not hold himself previously. Praise God.*

> **You are supposed to be in command as a child of God. Being a child of God makes you a solution.**

I will like you to move about with the consciousness that you are a solution.

For the earnest expectation of the creature waiteth for the manifestation of the sons of God -Roman 8:19

You are a solution and the world is waiting for you to manifest the power of God as a child of God.

Elias was a man subject to like passions as we are and he prayed earnestly that it might not rain: and it rained not on the earth by the space of three years and six months.

-James 5:17

Elias (Elijah) was a man that has demonstrated the power of God. He was able to control rain because he prayed earnestly. Earnest prayer precedes supernatural manifestation. He got the power to control the forces of nature through prayer. Right now my spirit is charged up and I want you to receive this charging of the Holy Spirit too. Today we witness all manner of disaster and it seems there is no one to take command. Earthquakes, tornados, flood etc is a common plaque today and the church of God is sleeping. Elijah was not a spirit he was a man like you and I. He was a man that knew his God and who he was in God.

> **You are always meeting with disappointment because you are combining falsehood with prayer.**

He believed God to the point that the ravens feed him. When last have you trusted in God for a supernatural supply? All what you do is to forge certificate and curriculum vitae so that you can get job. You are always meeting with disappointment because you are combining falsehood with prayer.

You got to stop making things your own way and depend on the will of God.

> **You got to stop making things your own way and depend on the will of God. My decision has been, whatever God cannot do let it remains undone.**

My decision has been, whatever God cannot do let it remains undone. God will be silent on you in as much as you're struggling your own way.

God's ways are not your ways and His thoughts are not your thoughts. As you stop depending on your own will and begin to depend on the will of God, He is going to send the ravens to you like Elijah if no one is ready. We have to dare trust in God for all supply;

> **When you operate in the Spirit of God what affects others will never affect you.**

Get thee hence, and turn thee eastward, and hide thyself by the brook Cherith, that is before Jordan. And it shall be, that thou shalt drink of the brook; and I have commanded the ravens to feed thee there.

-1King 17:3-4

Elijah decreed that there will be neither rain nor dew and it happened according to his words (1 King 17:1). The whole land was dry but he wasn't affected because he was operating in the Spirit of God. When you operate in the Spirit of God what affects others will never affect you. Kingdom prosperity is real! The world economy is going down. Tune into your radio or television channels and all you hear is bad news but I could assure you that you can escape all this austerity if you are operating according to the power and the dictates of the Holy Spirit. The only way to end poverty, austerity and challenges of your life is to obey and operate in the power of the Holy Spirit.

God said to Elijah, get on and turn eastward and hide by the brook Cherith that is before Jordan. This is what we call divine direction! You need to be intimate and operating in God's power to be able to hear vividly from him.

You are not suffering because you have no man neither because you lack one thing or the other but because you lack the anointing to hear the voice and the instruction of the Holy Spirit. God said to Peter cast your net into the deep for a harvest of fish after toiling all night;

And he said unto them, Cast the net on the right side of the ship, and ye shall find. They cast therefore, and now they were not able to draw it for the multitude of fishes.

- John 21:6

You can live in abundance if you can listen to God. There is a place God has commanded your blessing to be. Operating in the power of God is what give you access to hear from God like Elijah. To Peter, Jesus said, cast your net on the right side of the ship. To Elijah He gave him direction of the place He has commanded the raven to feed him. God has given a commandment concerning your case but you probably lack the spiritual sensitivity to hear from God. *Spiritual sensitivity is a product of spiritual development and empowerment. Spiritual empowerment is only possible when you operate with the Spirit of God and that is what keeps you in command.*

> **You are not suffering because you have no man neither because you lack one thing or the other but because you lack the anointing to hear the voice and the instruction of the Holy Spirit.**

And the word of the LORD came unto him, saying, Arise, get thee to Zarephath, which belongeth to Zidon, and dwell there: behold, I have commanded a widow woman there to sustain thee. So he arose and went to Zarephath. And when he came to the gate of the city, behold, the widow woman was there gathering of sticks: and he called to her, and said, Fetch me, I pray thee, a little water in a vessel, that I may drink. And as she was going to fetch it, he called to her, and said, Bring me, I pray thee, a morsel of bread in thine hand. And she said, As the LORD thy God liveth, I have not a cake, but an handful of meal in a barrel, and a little oil in a cruse: and, behold, I am gathering two sticks, that I may go in and dress it for me and my son, that we may eat it, and die. And Elijah said unto her, Fear not; go and do as thou hast said: but make me thereof a little cake first, and bring it unto me, and after make for thee and for thy son. For thus saith the LORD God of Israel, The barrel of meal shall not waste, neither shall the cruse of oil fail, until the day that the LORD sendeth rain upon the earth. And she went and did according to the saying of Elijah: and she, and he, and her house, did eat many days And the barrel of meal wasted not, neither did the cruse of oil fail, according to the word of the LORD, which he spake by Elijah

-1King 17:8-16

This is power in operation! But what is the key to this power? It is because he listened to God. *How can one hear from God? God is a Spirit and Elijah was a man with flesh and blood as you and I. How then could he hear from God? It means that he had to connect with the Spirit of God through his spirit to be able to hear from God.* For you to be able to connect with the Spirit of God through your spirit you will have to eliminate background noise so that your spirit can communicate with God. Any time you are on your knees, you are actually eliminating the background noise (Flesh), so that your spirit can talk with God;

God is a Spirit: and they that worship him must worship him in spirit and in truth.

-John 4:24

98

Whenever provision finished depends on God for another, He is always able. When the brook dried up, God has to relocate Elijah to the widow of Zeraphat. God can use anyone or anything at anytime in anyplace.

> Your blessing probably did not lie at where you are looking...... opportunity with God may not be what you take to be opportunity

Your blessing probably did not lie at where you are looking. Today people are too good in running after so called opportunity but opportunity with God may not be what you take to be opportunity. Of all people in the city God only send Elijah to a widow.

You do not need everyone in your life; you only need the right person. You do not need the president or so called rich people; you only need those that the Lord has sent. Anyone God has sent into your life will have all what it takes to sustain you, which is why you got to thank God for your wife, husband and your loved ones. Many people are having challenges today because they are running after the so-called glittering things, which are not necessarily gold. They feed themselves with what they never need. God knows what you need.

The place God has kept your own blessing may not have any form of glittering that your carnal sight will recognise and that's why it is necessary for you to be and remain in the Spirit. Walking in the Spirit increases your spiritual sensitivity to see things from God's own perspectives. Exploits are only possible when you see things the way God see them. The word of God is a Spirit (*pneuma*). You don't expect it to work according to your carnal expectation. It only works through spiritual mechanism which most times may seem foolish to the carnal mind.

> **You do not need the president or so called rich people; you only need those that the lord has sent. Anyone God has sent into your life will have all what it takes to sustain you**

Elijah's declaration worked through Spirit mechanism. The woman would have hardly thought of what she saw. I pity those that always think how will it be possible? Many time people sows is because they perceive the possibility of harvest; let me give $1000 may be the bank will clear that debt. You see the probability or possibility of debt cancellation before giving a $1000. You can't bribe God? Why don't you give that money and let God bless you through the Spirit mechanism. He may decide to bless you with $1,000,000 days after than cancelling the debt, as at you want it. Never think how your harvest will come. You sow in expectation but never think how your expectation will come to pass.

The words of Elijah were so powerful; the barrel of meal did not waste and the cruse of oil did not fail according to his words.

Elijah did the miracle of multiplication, similar with what Jesus did with two fishes and five loaves of bread because they were operating under the same Spirit.

You operate in the realm of possibility whenever you operate in the Spirit of God. I believe that God sent Elijah into the life of this widow to also turn things around for her.

> **Whenever God wants to turn things around for you he will always want you to act in faith by asking you to do the seemingly impossible things.**

Whenever God wants to turn things around for you he will always want you to act in faith by asking you to do the seemingly impossible things. *There was a time God told my wife and me to take all our money at home and in the bank to a church and we did and since then we begin to operate in divine prosperity.*

God told Elijah to go to the widow of Zarephath but God did not tell him to declare prosperity into her life. Elijah was simply operating in his prophetic or apostolic authority when he was making that declaration. *Every true man of God that truly operates with the Spirit of God operates with apostolic authority*. Elijah has demonstrated his apostolic authority several times that I can only mention some of them.

Then the king sent unto him a captain of fifty with his fifty. And he went up to him: and, behold, he sat on the top of an hill. And he spake unto him, Thou man of God, the king hath said, Come down. And Elijah answered and said to the captain of fifty, If I be a man of God, then let fire come down from heaven, and consume thee and thy fifty. And there came down fire from heaven, and consumed him and his fifty. Again also he sent unto him another captain of fifty with his fifty. And he answered and said unto him, O man of God, thus hath the king said, Come down quickly. And Elijah answered and said unto them, If I be a man of God, let fire come down from heaven, and consume thee and thy fifty. And the fire of God came down from heaven, and consumed him and his fifty. nd he sent again a captain of the third fifty with his fifty. And the third captain of fifty went up, and came and fell on his knees before Elijah, and besought him, and said unto him, O man of God, I pray thee, let my life, and the life

of these fifty thy servants, be precious in thy sight.
Behold, there came fire down from heaven, and burnt
up the two captains of the former fifties with their
fifties: therefore let my life now be precious in thy
sight.

-2 King 1:9-14

This is again a demonstration of apostolic authority. God
did not say Elijah call fire on
them. He decided to call the
fire down. I want you to
understand that this is literal
fire. He called down fire
from heaven. Anointing does
not beg! Those who are truly

> **Anointing does not beg! Those who are truly empowered cannot be a prey in the hand of the devil.**

empowered cannot be a prey in the hand of the devil.
Today the so-called believers appease the devil but true
believers sends fire upon the devil.

The devil has left me alone for long now and God is my
witness. The devil understands the blow and the trouble
he will have if he dear comes around me, so he prefer

104

not coming at all. The devil can only scratch in places where the ground is soft for him. Elijah called fire down twice until they began to plead with him.

Every child of God should have the potential to demonstrate the power of God. While we should not call fire down upon our

That affliction may not like to go except you release fire of God on it,

fellow human beings in this generation of grace, we can call fire down upon the works of the devil and the powers of darkness. You can call fire down upon cancer, asthma, HIV/AIDS, epilepsy, hypertension, diabetes, heart attacks, insanity, marital delay, unemployment, poverty, depression etc.

Know that the power of the Holy Spirit is the destructive power against the kingdom of darkness.

And when his disciples James and John saw this, they said, Lord, wilt thou that we command fire to come down from heaven, and consume them, even as Elias did? But he turned, and rebuked them, and said, Ye know not what manner of spirit ye are of. For the Son of man is not come to destroy men's lives, but to save them. And they went to another village.

-Luke 9:54-56.

Do you know that peter and John would have literally called down fire if not that Jesus stopped them? Firstly, they knew they have gotten the power to call down fire. Secondly Jesus knows that they can and that is why he said to them, do you not know the Spirit that you carry? Jesus said He did not come to destroy men's lives, but to save them. *Know that your sickness and challenges is not a man's life, it is devils lies and you can send fire on them The devil and demons are not men's lives either so, fell free to release the fire.* Anything that destroys the life of men is not of God and such things are all qualified for the consuming fire of God. That affliction may not like to go except you release fire of God on it, but you need to be empowered to be able to draw fire down.

And it came to pass, as they still went on, and talked, that, behold, there appeared a chariot of fire, and

106

horses of fire, and parted them both asunder; and Elijah went up by a whirlwind into heaven.-"

-King 2:11

Elijah lived the life of fire and was taken to heaven in chariots of fire and whirlwind. He was a man accustomed with fire. He indeed had the baptism of fire. This fire and whirlwind signifies the company of the Holy Spirit.

The mantle of Elijah was then passed on to Elisha.

Elisha

As I write this book, I became more aware of the awesome power that has been made available through the operation of the Spirit.

And he took the mantle of Elijah that fell from him, and smote the waters, and said, Where is the LORD God of Elijah? and when he also had smitten the waters, they parted hither and thither: and Elisha went over.

-2 King 2:14

Please think about this above story again! A mantle divided the waters, how deep is this water? This must be a river, as he could not cross. The mantle of Elijah is the Spirit of God in symbol. The power of God was heavy on it. It was this power that was also at work in Moses rod. It is a diving force. It is the same power in your mouth; the word of faith for the word of God is quick, powerful, piercing and dividing. The Word is unstoppable!

And when the sons of the prophets which were to view at Jericho saw him, they said, The spirit of Elijah doth rest on Elisha. And they came to meet him, and bowed themselves to the ground before him.

-2 King 2:15

The sons of the prophet looking at Elisha quickly understand that the Spirit of Elijah has rested upon

Elisha. This is what is called the transfer of anointing. If you are truly anointed people will know. Anointing cannot be hidden, it is meant for a show, a show of the devil's weaknesses and failures and a show of the praise of God.

And the men of the city said unto Elisha, Behold, I pray thee, the situation of this city is pleasant, as my lord seeth: but the water is naught, and the ground barren. And he said, Bring me a new cruse, and put salt therein. And they brought it to him. And he went forth unto the spring of the waters, and cast the salt in there, and said, thus saith the LORD, I have healed these waters; there shall not be from thence any more death or barren land. So the waters were healed unto this day, according to the saying of Elisha which he spake.

-2 King 2:19-22

The power of God is the cure for death and barrenness. The waters were permanently healed unto this day. It is only the power of God that brings permanent solution. Surgeon will only cut away your body but the power of God can heal you permanently. If you had put the time you waste moving about in search for solution into prayer, your life would have been changed by now.

> **Surgeons will only cut away your body but the power of God can heal you permanently**

Situation and people cannot embarrass those that are in command.

And he went up from thence unto Bethel: and as he was going up by the way, there came forth little children out of the city, and mocked him, and said unto him, Go up, thou bald head; go up, thou bald head. And he turned back, and looked on them, and cursed them in the name of the LORD. And there came forth two she bears out of the wood, and tare forty and two children of them.

-2 king 2:23-24

> **When power is in operation solutions rushes out.**

When you curse that situation in your life a greater power will appear and consume it. Could you imagine two she bear coming out of the wood? Was this a coincidence? Never! It is the power of God. The power of God released those bears. When power is in operation solutions rushes out.

The power of God in Elisha made the enemy (Moabites) to perceive water as blood and they suffer great defeat.

For thus saith the LORD, Ye shall not see wind, neither shall ye see rain; yet that valley shall be filled with water, that ye may drink, both ye, and your cattle, and your beasts...... And they rose up early in the morning, and the sun shone upon the water, and the Moabites saw the water on the other side as red as blood:

- 2 King 3:17 &22.

The Moabite perceive the water that God has provided for the people to drink as blood, thinking that the Israelites were all dead. The Moabites were deceived and

111

when they came for the spoil the Israelites attacked them severely. *The power of God can so cloth you that the enemy will begin to perceive you as a lion. They cannot come near you because they are not seeing an ordinary man. They are seeing a lion. The power of God can change people's perception about you. The power of God can turn that hatred to love, failure to success and poverty to wealth. The extent of your challenge does not matter when power comes. The Power of God is a transforming force. The power of God can cloth your business, houses, children and all that you have that the enemy cannot come near because all they could see is; Danger! Danger!! Danger!!!*

Power of God is the solution to everything. Elisha was operating in God's dimension of power because the Spirit of God was upon him. He was a solution to the challenges of people because the power of God is in operation in him.

Now there cried a certain woman of the wives of the sons of the prophets unto Elisha, saying, Thy servant my husband is dead; and thou knowest that thy servant did fear the LORD: and the creditor is come to take unto him my two sons to be bondmen. And Elisha said unto her, What shall I do for thee? tell me, what hast thou in the house? And she said, Thine handmaid hath not anything in the house, save a pot of oil. Then he said, Go, borrow thee vessels abroad of all thy neighbours, even empty vessels; borrow not a few. And when thou art come in, thou shalt shut the door upon thee and upon thy sons, and shalt pour out into all those vessels, and thou shalt set aside that which is full. So she went from him, and shut the door upon her and upon her sons, who brought the vessels to her; and she poured out. And it came to pass, when the vessels were full, that she said unto her son, Bring me yet a vessel. And he said unto her, there is not a vessel more. And the oil stayed. Then she came and told the man of God. And he said, Go, sell the oil, and pay thy debt, and live thou and thy children of the rest.

-2King4: 1-7

There are so many cries today but unfortunately, what most people do now is not to proffer solution but to encourage and send condolence. Elisha was a solution to this woman because he paid the cost of power. *When the power of God is upon you, supernatural multiplication is the result*. It is the power of God that makes this oil to swell and to keep swelling until the vessel finished and the multiplication stopped. A drop of oil was turned to

> **The power of God can transform your small business into a company if you can make room for the Holy Ghost and obey spiritual command**

an oil company; the power of God can transform your small business into a company if you can make room for the Holy Ghost and obey spiritual command. The power of God is a swelling force. It is a moving force. You got to make room available for it to move. The power of God can be present but unfelt if adequate provisions for His manifestation are not in place. Until you make room for Him you cannot feel Him.

As I read the scripture, I could see that the power of the Holy Spirit at work in a man is the solution to everything. Elisha prophecies never fall to the ground, he prophesied that the Shunemite woman will have a son and it happened. He also brought that child back to life when the woman ran to him that her child was dead (2 Kings 4:35-37). The power of the Holy Spirit is what give your words power and I cannot be tired of mentioning that again and again. It is the power that gives life; it is the quickening power, the power that translates from death to life.

And it fell on a day, that Elisha passed to Shunem, where was a great woman; and she constrained him to eat bread. And so it was, that as oft as he passed by, he turned in thither to eat bread. And she said unto her husband, Behold now, I perceive that this is an holy man of God, which passeth by us continually. Let us make a little chamber, I pray thee, on the wall; and let us set for him there a bed, and a table, and a stool, and a candlestick: and it shall be, when he cometh to us, that he shall turn in thither. And it fell on a day, that he came thither, and he turned into the chamber, and lay there. And he said to Gehazi his servant, Call this Shunammite. And when he had called her, she stood before him. And he said unto him, Say now unto her, Behold, thou hast been careful for us with all this care; what is to be done for thee? wouldest thou be spoken for to the king, or to the captain of the host? And she answered, I dwell among mine own people. And he said, What then is to be done for her? And Gehazi answered, Verily she hath no child, and her husband is old. And he said, Call her. And when he had called her, she stood in the door. And he said, About this season, according to the time of life, thou shalt embrace a son. And she said, Nay, my lord, thou man of God, do not lie unto thine handmaid. And the woman conceived, and bares a son at that season that Elisha had said unto her, according to the time of life.

- 2 King 4:8-17

Nothing is wrong with your body, nothing is wrong with your health, you do not have a child because your organs are bad or because you have passed menopause; it is because you lack the power of God. Menopause cannot stop the people of God from having children. I have seen a woman of 68 year old who has been married for about 36 years gave birth to a baby boy. Your situation is only because you have no power and you have no access to power. It will be easier for one to gain power of your own than looking for it elsewhere. It is easier to go to God than man.

> **Nothing is wrong with your body, nothing is wrong with your health, you do not have a child because your organs are bad or because you have passed menopause; it is because you lack the power of God.**

You do not need transportation money to talk to God neither do you need air time. What I think you need is time to persistently pray on your knee. There is no situation that can withstand the fire of the Holy Spirit.

Every child of God that has true fellowship with the Holy Spirit still lives in the Garden of Eden that God had originally designed for us. It is possible for you to live the easy and peaceful life; you can end incessant depression and challenges of your life by tapping into the power house of God.

> **. Every child of God that has true fellowship with the Holy Spirit still lives in the Garden of Eden that God had originally designed for us.**

Time will fail me to keep writing about the exploits of Elisha but let see one more demonstration of divine power that was at work in Him;

And the sons of the prophets said unto Elisha, Behold now, the place where we dwell with thee is too strait for us. Let us go, we pray thee, unto Jordan, and take thence every man a beam, and let us make us a place there, where we may dwell. And he answered, Go ye. And one said, Be content, I pray thee, and go with thy servants. And he answered, I will go. So he went with them. And when they came to Jordan, they cut down wood. But as one was felling a beam, the axe head fell into the water: and he cried, and said, Alas, master! for it was borrowed. And the man of God said, Where fell it? And he shewed him the place. And he cut down a stick, and cast it in thither; and the iron did swim. Therefore said he, Take it up to thee. And he put out his hand, and took

-2 Kings 6:1-7

The ministry of Elisha had so grown that the tent can no longer contain the sons of the prophets that they needed expansion. They requested for permission to go and build another and they were wise enough to invite the man of God to come along with them because they knew he is in the power of God.

Some fellows that you see are not just ordinary human beings; they are power of God personified. Look at what Elisha did when the borrowed axe fell into the water. A stick thrown into water

> **It really does not matter how long your situation has lasted or what you are going through right now, solution will come if only you can connect with the power of God.**

caused an axe to float? The stick should have flowed away, but it was not just a stick, it was the magnetic power of God.

Every tool from the hand of God is a magnetic power of God. This magnetic power of God in the form of a stick draws the axe from the bottom of the river. When you connect with the power of God it will draw you from every evil situation. You will only live in trouble if you are carnal and powerless. It really does not matter how long your situation has lasted or what you are going through right now, solution will come if only you can connect with the power of God. You have ability within

120

you to transform dry bones to giants if you can connect
with the power that activates prophetic words to action.

Ezekiel

*The hand of the LORD was upon me, and carried me
out in the spirit of the LORD, and set me down in the
midst of the valley which was full of bones, And caused
me to pass by them round about: and, behold, there
were very many in the open valley; and, lo, they were
very dry. And he said unto me, Son of man, can these
bones live? And I answered, O Lord GOD, thou
knowest Again he said unto me, Prophesy upon these
bones, and say unto them, O ye dry bones, hear the
word of the LORD. Thus saith the Lord GOD unto
these bones; Behold, I will cause breath to enter into
you, and ye shall live: And I will lay sinews upon you,
and will bring up flesh upon you, and cover you with
skin, and put breath in you, and ye shall live; and ye
shall know that I am the LORD. So I prophesied as I
was commanded: and as I prophesied, there was a
noise, and behold a shaking, and the bones came
together, bone to his bone. And when I beheld, lo, the*

sinews and the flesh came up upon them, and the skin covered them above: but there was no breath in them. Then said he unto me, Prophesy unto the wind, prophesy, son of man, and say to the wind, Thus saith the Lord GOD; Come from the four winds, O breath, and breathe upon these slain, that they may live. So I prophesied as he commanded me, and the breath came into them, and they lived, and stood up upon their feet, an exceeding great army. Then he said unto me, Son of man, these bones are the whole house of Israel: behold, they say, Our bones are dried, and our hope is lost: we are cut off for our parts.

-Ezekiel 37:1-11

Today men walk as trees because there is no life in them. Hypertension and heart attack is a common illness in our days because men's heart is beginning to fail them. Answer can never come until we activate and demonstrate the power of God.

The hand of the Lord was upon Ezekiel and that same hand carried him in the Spirit of the LORD. Those that are truly anointed by God move in the Spirit of God.

> **God can do everything but needed men to prophecy, men that are full of the Holy Spirit and power.**

God set Ezekiel to the valley of very dry bones and asked him a question; can these dry bones live? God is asking you the same question; do you think you can get out of that situation? God is simply saying to you; do you know you can prophecy life into your situation, do you really realize that something will happen when you prophecy, do you realize that the solution is in your mouth? God can do everything but needed men to prophecy, men that are full of the Holy Spirit and power. You will not know what God can do until you prophecy in the power of God. The Lord told Ezekiel what to say, and he prophesied as commanded. When last have you heard God so clear? It is not a challenge for those in the Spirit to hear from God.

Are you surprise that you are born again and cannot hear from God? You need not to! Because when you are born again you still need to learn how to recognise the voice of God. You will need to read the book I wrote on how to hear from God. Samuel was righteous but has to learn how to recognise God's voice through his mentor, Eli. There are things you need to learn because knowledge is not a gift. It is a deliberate effort to know and you must labour to know.

You can only begin to hear the voice of God if you talk to him often. The more of time you spend with God the more of his voice you hear and the more powerful you become.

It is only prophecy that is declared according to the word of God that materialise. When Ezekiel began to prophecy as commanded, the very dry bones become exceedingly great army. We could understand from the scripture that these dry bones are the houses of Israel. If you are truly anointed, you can prophecy your loved once into the kingdom of God as exceedingly great army.

You need power to oversee the church; you need power to be successful in your business. You need power to rule your house; you need power to be able to drive away evil Spirit.

David

And David spake to the men that stood by him, saying, What shall be done to the man that killeth this Philistine, and taketh away the reproach from Israel? for who is this uncircumcised Philistine, that he should defy the armies of the living God?.... And David said to Saul, Let no man's heart fail because of him; thy servant will go and fight with this Philistine. And Saul said to David, Thou art not able to go against this Philistine to fight with him: for thou art but a youth, and he a man of war from his youth. And David said unto Saul, Thy servant kept his father's sheep, and there came a lion, and a bear, and took a lamb out of the flock: And I went out after him, and smote him, and delivered it out of his mouth: and when he arose against me, I caught him by his beard, and smote him, and slew him.Thy servant slew both the lion and the bear: and this uncircumcised Philistine shall be as one of them, seeing he hath defied the armies of the living God. David said moreover, The LORD that delivered me out of the paw of the lion, and out of the paw of the bear, he will deliver me out of the hand of this Philistine. And Saul said unto David, Go, and the LORD be with thee. And Saul armed David with his armour, and he put an helmet of brass upon his head; also he armed him with a coat of mail. And David girded his sword upon his armour, and he assayed to go; for he had not proved it. And David said unto Saul, I cannot go with these; for I have not proved them. And David put them off him. And he took his staff in his hand, and chose him five smooth stones out of the brook, and put them in a shepherd's bag which he had, even in a scrip; and his sling was in his hand: and he drew near to the Philistine..........Then said David to the Philistine, Thou comest to me with a sword, and with a spear, and with a shield: but I come to thee in the name of the LORD of hosts, the God of the armies of Israel, whom thou hast defied. And all this assembly shall know that the LORD saveth not with sword and spear:

for the battle is the LORD'S, and he will give you into our hands. And David put his hand in his bag, and took thence a stone, and slang it, and smote the Philistine in his forehead, that the stone sunk into his forehead; and he fell upon his face to the earth. So David prevailed over the Philistine with a sling and with a stone, and smote the Philistine, and slew him; but there was no sword in the hand of David.

-1Samuel 17:26, 32-40, 45, 47,

The exploit of David would have not been possible without the power of the Holy Spirit. The Spirit of the Lord came upon David when Samuel anointed him.

Then Samuel took the horn of oil, and anointed him in the midst of his brethren: and the Spirit of the LORD came upon David from that day forward. So Samuel rose up, and went to Ramah.

-1Samuel 16:13

It is not ordinary for a man to kill a lion and a bear with an ordinary hand. That is the power of the Holy Spirit (anointing). The power of the Holy

> **Whatever the LORD has done for you in the past is to increase your faith for the future.**

Spirit can so energise us physically for strength. Anointing is what makes an ordinary man to do the extraordinary. David realised that it is with the help of God that he was able to kill a lion and a bear and so he believe that he will deal with Goliath (the uncircumcised Philistine) that want to defile the army of the living God.

Whatever the LORD has done for you in the past is to increase your faith for the future. David faith was encouraged and that is why his focus was on the bigness of God than the big size of Goliath. *The Holy Spirit will amplify your faith above your situation in Jesus name.* David was dressed with armours of war but he could not make use of them because he has not tried them, the only thing David has tried was his confidence in God.

The Holy Spirit builds your confidence on God rather than on physical weapon. He conquered Goliath without those physical weapons. He prophetically picked five stone, which I believe represents the name of JESUS. Jesus is the power and the wisdom of God that was at work in David and that is why he silenced those that want to defile the army of the living God. The only way you can challenge those situation that wants to defile you is through the anointing of the Holy Spirit. The power of the Holy Spirit is above physical power and weapon. *The most important thing I crave for is the anointing.*

> **The only way you can challenge those situation that wants to defile you is through the anointing of the Holy Spirit.**

129

Daniel

Forasmuch as an excellent spirit, and knowledge, and understanding, interpreting of dreams, and shewing of hard sentences, and dissolving of doubts, were found in the same Daniel, whom the king named Belteshazzar: now let Daniel be called, and he will shew the interpretation.

-Daniel 5:12

The Spirit of God is an excellent Spirit. Whenever the Spirit of God is in operation excellence will be in place, it is the Spirit of understanding and knowledge, it is the Spirit that reveals secrets and mysteries, and it is the Spirit of faith because it dissolves all doubt. Daniel was operating in the power of the Spirit of God and he was widely consulted. People will always consult those that are filled with the Spirit of God. Daniel lived the life of excellence because the Spirit of excellence was in him. He was filled with understanding of secrets and mysteries of God. Daniel prophesied the end time and that is what is helping us to understand the contemporary events today.

Daniels was so preferred than his colleagues because of the presence of God in his life.

Then this Daniel was preferred above the presidents and princes, because an excellent spirit was in him; and the king thought to set him over the whole realm

-Daniel 6:3

The power of the Holy Spirit is what makes you to be preferred above other people. This is because this power drives excellence in you and every one will like to associate with excellent things. The Holy Spirit is what helps you to live a beautiful life.

Minor Prophets

All the Minor Prophets from Hosea to Malachi operated under the influence of the Holy Ghost. It is with this anointing that Joel prophesied the outpouring of the Holy Spirit upon the Church.

And it shall come to pass afterward, that I will pour out my spirit upon all flesh; and your sons and your daughters shall prophesy, your old men shall dream dreams, your young men shall see visions: And also upon the servants and upon the handmaids in those days will I pour out my spirit.

-Joel 2:28-29

Amos prophesied that there would be an outpouring of the Holy Spirit in a greater measure than what they have experienced in the Old Testament. The prophecy of Amos is so accurate and spans from generation to generation that will ever be saved. This prophecy has been fulfilling right from generation to generation. It was fulfilled on the day of Pentecost and it is still in fulfilment.

And it shall come to pass in the last days, saith God, I will pour out of my Spirit upon all flesh: and your sons and your daughters shall prophesy, and your young men shall see visions, and your old men shall dream dreams: And on my servants and on my handmaidens I will pour out in those days of my Spirit; and they shall prophesy:

-Acts 2:17-18

Jesus confirmed this prophecy when He promised the church that He will send the Holy Spirit.

And, behold, I send the promise of my Father upon you: but tarry ye in the city of Jerusalem, until ye be endued with power from on high.

-Luke 24:49

Some people today said no more Holy Spirit baptism, no more speaking in tongues. That is heresy! The promise is also for everyone that will ever be born again or called into the kingdom of God with the same manifestation of power and evidence of speaking in tongues.

For the promise is unto you, and to your children, and to all that are afar off, even as many as the Lord our God shall call

-Acts 2:39

Habakkuk also prophesied the growth of the end time church by the anointing of the Holy Spirit;

For the earth shall be filled with the knowledge of the glory of the LORD, as the waters cover the sea.

-Habbakkuk 2:14

I believe that you and I will again experience the power of the Holy Spirit mightily before the rapture. Our generation is so wicked that we need to be empowered to overcome the harassment of the devil and to put Satan's kingdom down.

Jesus being the Son of God could not do without the power of the Holy Spirit.

Jesus

And there was delivered unto him the book of the prophet Esaias. And when he had opened the book, he found the place where it was written, The Spirit of the Lord is upon me, because he hath anointed me to

134

preach the gospel to the poor; he hath sent me to heal the broken hearted, to preach deliverance to the captives, and recovering of sight to the blind, to set at liberty them that are bruised, To preach the acceptable year of the Lord. And he closed the book, and he gave it again to the minister, and sat down. And the eyes of all them that were in the synagogue were fastened on him.

-Luke 4:17-20

The ministry of Jesus was so successful because of the power of the Holy Spirit. He entered into the temple and read the promise of God concerning His life. The healing ministry of Jesus, His wisdom dimension and the power with which He preached were possible through the anointing of the Holy Spirit.

How God anointed Jesus of Nazareth with the Holy Ghost and with power: who went about doing good, and healing all that were oppressed of the devil; for God was with him.

-Acts 10:38

135

Jesus went about doing good because God anointed him with the Holy Ghost and with power. The healing and deliverance ministry of Jesus is because the power of God was at work in Him.

> **Anyone that truly has the anointing of the Holy Spirit at work in him/her such is worthy to be heard.**

Jesus kind of result is always possible if we operate in that same dimension of anointing.

The ministry of Jesus received open approval when the Holy Spirit fell on him. People flood to hear Jesus speak because God approved His ministry. If God truly anoints your ministry people will not be lacking in the church. *I was praying some time ago in the year 2010 and God said to me if I give you words to speak I would bring people that will listen to what I have given you to speak.* God openly declared that Jesus is

> **If God truly anoints your ministry people will not be lacking in the church.**

worthy to be heard because He has the anointing of the Holy Spirit at work in Him. Anyone that truly has the anointing of the Holy Spirit at work in him/her such is worthy to be heard;

While he yet spake, behold, a bright cloud overshadowed them: and behold a voice out of the cloud, which said, This is my beloved Son, in whom I am well pleased; **hear ye him**.

-Matthew 17:5. (Bold; mine)

And it came to pass in those days that Jesus came from Nazareth of Galilee, and was baptized of John in Jordan. And straightway coming up out of the water, he saw the heavens opened, and the Spirit like a dove descending upon him: And there came a voice from heaven, saying, Thou art my beloved Son, in whom I am well pleased.

–Mark 1:9-11

This is an open confirmation of the presence of the Holy Spirit upon Jesus. If Jesus can be baptised with the Holy

Spirit needless to say how important it is for you and I. The ministry of the apostles were so effective because of the power of the Holy Spirit.

Peter

You must have read how peter was full of fear and denied Jesus three times because of fear. This same peter became so bold in declaring the gospel openly after the baptism of the Holy Spirit on the day of Pentecost and three thousand souls were won.

Now when they heard this, they were pricked in their heart, and said unto Peter and to the rest of the apostles, Men and brethren, what shall we do?......Then they that gladly received his word were baptized: and the same day there were added unto them about three thousand souls.

-Acts2: 37 & 41

Can you imagine 3000 souls being born again in one crusade with just one message? It is the anointing of the

Holy Ghost that brings conviction of sin; they were pricked in their heart when they heard the gospel. Three thousands souls were added to the church and it did not just stop there as the church continues to experience growth;

> **We need revival in today's church and it need to start from you.**

And they, continuing daily with one accord in the temple, and breaking bread from house to house, did eat their meat with gladness and singleness of heart. Praising God, and having favour with all the people. And the **Lord added to the church daily such as should be saved.**

-Acts 2:46-47(bolden mine)

The great revival in the New Testament church was attributed to the working power of the Holy Ghost. This you may know, but what have you done about it in improving today's church. If you are not concerned, it will never affect you.

Now Peter and John went up together into the temple at the hour of prayer, being the ninth hour. And a certain man lame from his mother's womb was carried, whom they laid daily at the gate of the temple which is called Beautiful, to ask alms of them that entered into the temple; Who seeing Peter and John about to go into the temple asked an alms. And Peter, fastening his eyes upon him with John, said, Look on us. And he gave heed unto them, expecting to receive something of them. Then Peter said, Silver and gold have I none; but such as I have give I thee: In the name of Jesus Christ of Nazareth rise up and walk. And he took him by the right hand, and lifted him up: and immediately his feet and ankle bones received strength. And he leaping up stood, and walked, and entered with them into the temple, walking, and leaping, and praising God. And all the people saw him walking and praising God:

- Acts 3:1-9

> **The apostles were able to live above money and exalt the power of God more than money.**

This is an open declaration of the power of God. The apostles were able to live above money and exalt the power of God more than money. The anointing of the Holy Spirit is more than money. It is the very easy way of living in abundance than running after money. You will actually be able to possess the entire world in prosperity and in righteousness for Christ Jesus if you actually pursue the power of the Holy Spirit more than money. The blessing of the Lord is not the money, cars, and other materials things. The blessing of the Lord is an anointing and when that anointing is on you everything will begin to work out for you. The money, car, health and all other material things is the outcome of the blessing just like the ragging sea is not the storm but the outcome of the storm. When you get the blessing the money will follow but you can get money without being blessed. People suffer so long because they are looking for money and material things more than the anointing.

The solution to your challenges is not in the material things. it is in the anointing.

The power of the Holy Spirit can raise you from your lunatic state to wealth, health, joy, and recognition. Right now I see you operating in that level in Jesus name. Seek the Holy Spirit and the anointing, it is only then that you can demonstrate power.

Peter and the rest apostle were no longer afraid any more. They now spoke boldly to the people before whom they were afraid previously. Peter can challenge even the crucifier of Jesus now;

And as they spake unto the people, the priests, and the captain of the temple, and the Sadducees, came upon them, Being grieved that they taught the people, and preached through Jesus the resurrection from the dead.............Then Peter, filled with the Holy Ghost, said unto them, Ye rulers of the people, and elders of Israel, Be it known unto you all, and to all the people of Israel, that by the name of Jesus Christ of Nazareth, whom ye crucified, whom God raised from the dead, even by him doth this man stand here before you whole. This is the stone which was set at nought of you builders, which is become the head of the corner. Neither is there salvation in any other: for there is none other name under heaven given among men, whereby we must be saved. And they called them, and commanded them not to speak at all nor teach in the name of Jesus. But Peter and John answered and said unto them, whether it be right in the sight of God to hearken unto you more than unto God, judge ye. For we cannot but speak the things which we have seen and heard.

-Acts 4:1-2,8, 10-12,18-20

Why are you ashamed of evangelism? Why is it that you do not want people to know that you are a child of God? You speak in tongue but you cannot evangelise, why? Who baptised you? Is it with the same baptism that the apostle had? Some of us are even ashamed to carry our bible, some are so happy now that they can now carry the electronic version of the bible in their phones and computers not because it may be easier for them but probably because they are ashamed to carry the bible. You can never be ashamed of the word of God if you both carry and know the power of God. It is those that both realize and carry the power of God that can demonstrate it.

For I am not ashamed of the gospel of Christ: for it is the power of God unto salvation to everyone that believeth; to the Jew first, and also to the Greek.

-Roman 1:16

Whosoever therefore shall be ashamed of me and of my words in this adulterous and sinful generation; of him also shall the Son of man be ashamed, when he cometh in the glory of his Father with the holy angels.

-Mark 8:38

We need to awake to the apostolic dimension of aggressive evangelism in this adulterous and sinful generation. If you are ashamed of the word of God, He will also be ashamed of you.

I was going out for evangelism at the age of about 10 with a friend who came to stay in our family house, as we were going, we meet a boy that knows my friend and he asked if my friend was carrying the bible and he quickly replied that it was a dictionary and not the bible.

If you are ashamed of the word of God, He will also be ashamed of you.

It is foolishness to be shameful of what is gainful. If you are truly baptised, you will not be ashamed of the gospel of Christ. You also need to teach your children about the power of God.

Philip

Then Philip went down to the city of Samaria, and preached Christ unto them. And the people with one accord gave heed unto those things which Philip spake, hearing and seeing the miracles which he did.

-Acts 8:5-6

The ministry of Philip was characterized with the power of God. Philip did not only preach the word of God but also demonstrate the power of God. Our preaching is to be accompanied by undeniable power of God. The gospel indeed is the power of God (Roman 1:16). The gospel of Christ = the power to **everyone** that believes (faith) in Jesus Christ. This is the universal formula for signs and wonders in ministry. Anywhere the gospel of Jesus Christ is being preached without power it means that faith is absent. This power demonstration that accompanies the gospel is not only for men of God or those with the gift of miracle, it is for **everyone** that is saying the 'Word' with faith. If you demonstrate the power of God your business will grow, if you demonstrate the power of God your ministry will grow and if you demonstrate the power of God heaven will be open over your life.

Ananias & Paul

And Ananias went his way, and entered into the house; and putting his hands on him said, Brother Saul, the Lord, even Jesus, that appeared unto thee in the way as

146

thou camest, hath sent me, that thou mightest receive thy sight, and be filled with the Holy Ghost. And immediately there fell from his eyes as it had been scales: and he received sight forthwith, and arose, and was baptized

-Acts 9:17-18

Why did Saul receive his sight? Ananias laid his hands of power on him before he can regain his sight back. When you carry the power of God it shows.

Saul who is called Paul was filled with the Holy Ghost immediately, which is why he did great exploit in the body of Christ. The teachings and miracle of Paul was so unique because of the power that was at work in him. His entire missionary journeys were made possible through the power of the Holy Spirit.

Paul spirit was stirred in him when he saw the city wholly given to idolatry. How do you feel when you see young people smoking on the street, how do you feel when you meet with atheists,...

Now while Paul waited for them at Athens, his spirit was stirred in him, when he saw the city wholly given to idolatry. Therefore disputed he in the synagogue with the Jews, and with the devout persons, and in the market daily with them that met with him

- Acts 17:16-17

Paul spirit was stirred in him when he saw the city wholly given to idolatry. How do you feel when you see young people smoking on the street, how do you feel when you meet with atheists, how do you fell when you see great number of the world population going after falsehood and how do you feel when you see that the church has lost value and power? Until your spirit man is stirred up nothing happens. You can only demonstrate power when you are filled with the Holy Ghost and jealous for the Lord God. You can only wake up in the night to pray when you feel concerned and stirred up in your inner man, you can only evangelize when your spirit is stirred up toward the lost souls. God will only use those that have the burden to see the move of God.

CHAPTER FOUR

POWER DIMENSIONS

People sometimes attribute the power of God to Satan when they see instantaneous miracle. So many have believed that God is slow to answering them and they carry the mentality that if it happens instantaneously is not God. People that have not experienced the power of God always think this way. Great numbers of people are used to being comforted in sorrow and in their sickness because there is no power to deliver them. God never wants us to take comfort in sorrow and in infirmity, they only time he comforts us in pain is when we suffer for his name's sake (persecution), which is for a moment. Paul calls it light affliction, which usually turns out for our good.

For our light affliction, which is but for a moment, worketh for us a far more exceeding and eternal weight of glory

- 2Corinthians 4:17

You are not born again to suffer. You are born to win. Winning as a child of God implies that you demonstrate His power with violent faith.

I want you to understand that the power of God is real. There are different dimension of the power of God and learn not to criticize if you are not familiar with any of them.

Healing power

There is no sickness that God cannot heal. God can cause an amputated leg to grow out again, He can bring out bullet from the body, and He can heal cancer, diabetes, stroke pile, and depression... God can heal all manner of sickness because He got all the power.

And Jesus came and spake unto them, saying, All power is given unto me in heaven and in earth.

-Matthew 28:18

Everyone that had ever come to Jesus gets healed and He is still in the healing business till today. Do not allow

151

people to deceive you that the time of miracle has past. Jesus is the same yesterday, today and forever.

Jesus Christ the same yesterday, and today, and forever.

-Hebrew 13:8

Jesus healed all that were oppressed of the devil because God was with Him. He did not just heal some but **all**. *How God anointed Jesus of Nazareth with the Holy Ghost and with power: who went about doing good, and* **healing all that were oppressed of the devil***; for God was with him.*

-Acts 10:38

I will like you to understand that the devil is the author of all sicknesses and diseases. It is Satan that afflicts people not God, some has misinterpreted the bible; though suffering is mentioned in the bible, it does not imply sickness; *If we suffer, we shall also reign with him: if we deny him, he also will deny us:*

-2 Timothy 2:12

If we suffer with Christ we will also reign with Him. What did Christ suffer: cancer, tuberculosis, and heart attack? Never! He suffered persecution. Everyone that will live the life of holiness will also suffer persecution.

Yea, and all that will live godly in Christ Jesus shall suffer persecution.

-2Timothy 3:12.

Jesus cannot use sickness to chasten us. I have heard people said this sickness or diseases are from God, No! God will never use sickness to chastise us. When God chastise us, He trains us to be a better person and not putting sickness upon us. The word chastise in Greek means to educate. The chastisement of God is meant to educate us in the ways and acts of God.

> **What you cannot believe God for you cannot receive.**

Stop using Job as an example, God did not put affliction on Job. satan caused the sickness of Job. Though Job fears God, he did not believe that God could deliver him from sickness. A lot of you

153

may be born again but still find it difficult to believe God for your healing. What you cannot believe God for you cannot receive.

For the thing which I greatly feared is come upon me, and that which I was afraid of is come unto me.

-Job3:25

> **No matter how righteous we might be we will not be able to please God without faith.**

I understand that though Job loves God, he was still afraid of sickness and destruction. No matter how righteous we might be we will not be able to please God without faith.

But without faith it is impossible to please him: for he that cometh to God must believe that he is, and that he is a rewarder of them that diligently seek him.

-Hebrew 11:6

God will never respond to your emotion, He responds to your faith. You can be a child of God and Satan will still torment you if you fail to put your faith in Him. I can understand from the word of God that the case of Job worsens because of his fear. Fear is what makes the devil to have access to Job and fear is also what made his situation worse. Let us listen to Job in his own words;

Fear came upon me, and trembling, which made all my bones to shake.

-Job 4:14

He was affected even to the bone because of fear. Fear actually kill and have killed a lot of people. Fear itself is a sickness because it can make all the bone of your body to shake. If fear can make the bones to shake let alone the flesh, it then means that fear can induce cancer in the flesh and cause incurable disease in the blood.

The doctor examined you and wrote in a sheet of paper the report that you have HIV/AIDS etc. and you accepted it. Jesus, the greatest physician also examined you and wrote in the most potent book, the Bible or through the Holy Spirit, said to you that you have no sickness or disease and you disbelieve him, why?

155

Who hath believed our report? and to whom is the arm of the LORD revealed?

-Isaiah 53:1

Until you believe you will not see the miracle of God. The first step to your miracle is to believe what God said more than what the doctor said to you. Believe God and disbelieve satan. Sicknesses and diseases are never of God.

One of the things that the church has grossly misunderstood today is the issue of the thorn in the life of Paul. The bible did not record that Paul's thorn was from God. Paul himself admits that the devil was the source of his thorn.

And lest I should be exalted above measure through the abundance of the revelations, there was given to me a thorn in the flesh, the messenger of Satan to buffet me, lest I should be exalted above measure. For this thing I besought the Lord thrice, that it might depart from me. And he said unto me, My grace is sufficient for thee: for my strength is made perfect in weakness. Most gladly therefore will I rather glory in my infirmities, that the power of Christ may rest upon me. Therefore I take pleasure in infirmities, in reproaches, in necessities, in persecutions, in distresses for Christ's sake: for when I am weak, then am I strong.

-2 Corinthians 12:7-10

Understand also that the bible did not call this thorn sickness. Paul said he sought the Lord thrice but the Lord said His grace is sufficient for him and his strength is made perfect in weakness (verse 8, 9), meaning that, that weakness cannot affect the ministry of Paul because of the grace of God. In other word the weakness in the flesh of Paul reveals the effectiveness of the power and strength at work in Paul. The intensity of light is revealed in darkness.

And the light shineth in darkness; and the darkness comprehended it not   *-John 1:5.*

Lights can only shine in darkness. Light is of no use without darkness. The value of the strength of Paul was revealed by the presence of his weakness (infirmity).

157

Understand also that this infirmity came for Christ's sake (verse 10), through preaching of Jesus Christ. The devil will always want to attack people that preach Jesus but his attack is of no value because His grace is sufficient for us and our strength is made perfect in weakness, meaning that the weakness is useless to us. I therefore declare every form of weakness in your life useless in Jesus mighty name.

It is wonderful to know that the God that we serve will not only deliver us from problems or what I will call challenges but proves us through them to show the devil that we are more than talking.

Many in their sicknesses and diseases look to God as the cause some said 'let give thanks for this is the will of God concerning us'. Well! Concerning them not me because I have not read in the bible where sicknesses and diseases is the will of God for a new covenant believer in this dispensation of grace. Let us look closely at the scripture they seem to misinterpret:

In everything give thanks: for this is the will of God in Christ Jesus concerning you

------------------------------------1Thessalonians 5:18

The above scripture did not say that your sicknesses and diseases is the will of God neither did it say that everything in your life is the will of God. The scripture here simply said that **thanksgiving** *is the will of God in Christ Jesus for your life. While that situation might not be the will of God in your life, the thanksgiving to God must be the will of God in your life.*

If you are sick or having one bad moment or the other and you are giving thanks to God, that thanksgiving is not because of that bad situation but because of the promise of better future that the Lord have for you.

For I know the thoughts that I think toward you, saith the LORD, thoughts of peace, and not of evil, to give you an expected end

------------------------------------ Jeremiah 29:11

Give thanks to God because He is making the way out for you while in that situation. God thought for you is how to bring you into your expectation and not to leave you in sicknesses, diseases or one challenges or the other.

God's thought for you is of peace and not of evil. Anything evil in your life is not of God, it is of the devil. All evil is of the devil. D-EVIL means Destructive Evil.

So, understand that thanksgiving is the will of God in Christ Jesus for you.

For ye have need of patience, that, after ye have done the will of God, ye might receive the promise.

Hebrews 10:36

What is the will of God that we have been discussing here? Thanksgiving of course! As you patiently do the will of God by giving thanks you will certainly receive all that the Lord has promised you in Jesus name.

> **Anointing to preach implies anointing for healing.**

Divine healing is real and one of the dimensions of the power of the Holy Spirit is healing. Jesus commanded us to both preach and heal. Today we use the issue of gifts as an excuses but I tell you that every one that is truly send by God to preach should be able to lay hand on the sick and the sick will recover. Anointing to preach implies anointing for healing.

And these signs shall follow them that believe; In my name shall they cast out devils; they shall speak with new tongues; They shall take up serpents; and if they drink any deadly thing, it shall not hurt them; they shall lay hands on the sick, and they shall recover. So then after the Lord had spoken unto them, he was received up into heaven, and sat on the right hand of God. And they went forth, and preached everywhere, the Lord working with them, and confirming the word with signs following. Amen.

- Mark 16:17-20

You can see that Jesus mentioned clearly that we will lay our hand upon the sick and the sick shall recover. That is power for healing. The power for healing actually comes through the indwelling of the Spirit of God that is why Jesus said they shall speak in new tongues which is the evidence of the Holy Ghost baptism.

Power to raise the dead

Jesus has the power to raise the dead because He is the firstborn from the dead;

And he is the head of the body, the church: who is the beginning, the firstborn from the dead; that in all things he might have the preeminence.

-Colosians 1:18

One might ask, how is he the firstborn from the dead knowing that He raised Lazarus from the dead before? He is the firstborn of the dead because all those that rose from the dead before and after him lived to die again but

He rose from the dead and He's alive for evermore, seated at the right hand of the father.

He has pre-eminence over death. Another dimension of the power of God is to raise the dead. So many people do not believe that the power of God can raise the dead. I have had one on one interaction with those that are dead and were back to life through the power of the Holy Spirit that is at work in the life of believers that prayed for them.

And when he thus had spoken, he cried with a loud voice, Lazarus, come forth. And he that was dead came forth, bound hand and foot with grave clothes: and his face was bound about with a napkin. Jesus saith unto them, loose him, and let him go. Then many of the Jews which came to Mary, and had seen the things which Jesus did, believed on him.

–John 11:43-45

Jesus raised Lazarus back to life even after He had been buried because He is the resurrection and the life.

But when Jesus heard it, he answered him, saying, Fear not: believe only, and she shall be made whole. And when he came into the house, he suffered no man to go in, save Peter, and James, and John, and the father and the mother of the maiden. And all wept, and bewailed her: but he said, Weep not; she is not dead, but sleepeth. And they laughed him to scorn, knowing that she was dead. And he put them all out, and took her by the hand, and called, saying, Maid, arise. And her spirit came again, and she arose straightway: and he commanded to give her meat. And her parents were astonished: but he charged them that they should tell no man what was done.

—Acts 8:50-56

Impossibility is the language of unbelief! They laughed

> **Impossibility is the language of unbelief!**

Jesus to scorn because they think that death is the end. Death with God is not the end but a bend. Jesus raised the dead and as many that believe can also raise the dead because the works of God must continue and because Jesus is no more on earth, he duplicates his Spirit upon us to do these works.

Verily, verily, I say unto you, He that believeth on me, the works that I do shall he do also; and greater works than these shall he do; because I go unto my Father.

-John 14:12

Late Archbishop Benson Idahosa said that when he was a teenager, his pastor preached that anyone that believes can raise the dead. His pastor that preached that message never raised any dead but Idahosa believed the word of God through his pastor and he took his bicycle and began to ride from house to house in the city of Benin, Nigeria. When he gets to each house he will shout, is there any dead here? Eventually he found one, a young lady that was dead, her name was Inuwata and he prayed and she came back to life. Since then God has used him to bring several people back to life.

This miracle was also common in the ministry of Bishop David Oyedepo. The church members testified of raising

165

the dead using mantles from him according to their testimonies that I personally heard.

The resurrection of the dead is another dimension of the Holy Ghost power. The resurrection of Jesus from the dead is a demonstration of his victory over death.

All children of God have power over death, meaning that we can control death.

Forasmuch then as the children are partakers of flesh and blood, he also himself likewise took part of the same; that through death he might destroy him that had the power of death, that is, the devil; And deliver them who through fear of death were all their lifetime subject to bondage

-Hebrews 2:14-15

The devil is the one that have the power of death prior to the death and resurrection of Jesus. Jesus has already destroyed the devil. Every victory of Jesus is also for the church. Death is no longer an issue and that is why the present day believer will again and again demonstrate power over death by bringing the dead back to life.

So when this corruptible shall have put on incorruption, and this mortal shall have put on immortality, then shall be brought to pass the saying that is written, **Death is swallowed up in victory**

-1Corinthians 15:54 (bolden, mine)

Understand that each time you operate in the Holy Spirit; you are operating in the incorruptible, which guarantees your victory over death. The anointing of the Holy Spirit in us is making a mess of death, for that reason, death cannot see us either through accident, sickness, riot and by any means because it has been swallowed up in victory. So, one of an outstanding miracle in the body of Christ today is deliverance from the dead and from death.

Power for creative miracles

There is what is called creative miracles. It is bringing what previously does not exist into existence with the power of God.

I was invited to a prayer meeting to pray for a couple that needed a baby. God revealed to me that the woman has no fallopian tube and she confirmed it when I asked her. I was in the Spirit and God showed me how the devil has stolen her fallopian tube. I read scriptures to her and prayed for her

God can replace any organ that is lacking or bad in your body and right now I command organ replacement in Jesus name.

After some months I heard that the woman was pregnant who has not been able to conceive previously.

God can replace any organ that is lacking or bad in your body and right now I command organ replacement in Jesus name.

Part of creative miracle is the creation of opportunities.

God can create opportunities

> **Whenever the Holy Spirit moves creative miracle is the result.**

like job, contracts and life partner for you. Creation of opportunity is also part of the dimension of the power of God.

Whenever the Holy Spirit moves creative miracle is the result. The Spirit of God was moving upon the face of the water that is why God said let there be light and there was light. Many people are insensitive to the move of God and that is why they hardly receive anything from God. If you want creative miracle to happen in your life make sure you create an atmosphere for the Holy Spirit to move in your life.

Today there are miracles of automatic weight loss, miracle money and miracle opportunity.

There was a brother by name Simeon, who was jobless several years after graduation. One day, I was praying in the bush and the Lord spoke to me; 'say to Simeon that Friday this week he will get a job'. I immediately rang him and told him. Throughout that week Simeon said he did not go out except on Friday evening after close of work as at 6p.m. As he was moving on the street, he came across an international establishment with security men at the gate, he approached them saying; sirs, I am looking for a job, do you know if there is any vacancy here? And they said, why coming now, the office is closed for the day but the manager is still inside, and they granted him access. Note that this young man did not even have an appointment with the manager. On getting to the manager, he simply said, sir, I am looking for job, I read accounting and I need a job. The manager immediately replied, my accountant has resigned and we need one, will you want to start now? Praise the Lord! That was a creative job, a creative miracle. In this very season you must experience a creative miracle in Jesus name.

When I was in the university, there was this brother that sensed and respects the anointing of God upon my life. He was on campus looking for admission to study law. At this time it was very difficult to get admission to

Nigerian university because of the competition and quota system. His university matriculation exam score was far from the score required for admission. One day this brother came to my room, that very day I cooked yam with 70% of pepper (a very hot spice) that I myself cannot even eat, I was contemplating how to finish the food when he walked into my room. I now said bro here is food but the pepper is too much to be eaten, will you eat? And I said, if you can eat this yam with me, I will pray for you and you will get the admission irrespective of your score. He accepted and managed to eat the yam. He was eating this yam and was sweating terribly. It was indeed a difficult thing to do but was simply obeying the dictate of a prophet of God. Few weeks later after eating the yam, the university senate met and they decided to bring out a 4th list of admission, which is unusual because as at then 3rd list is usually the final admission list. In that 4th list, he was admitted to read law. Praise the Lord!

God will create a future for you in Jesus name but learn to obey the instruction of prophets, *prophets are God's instruments of change and they must be believed and obeyed (2 Chronicles 20:20).* Spiritual command may seem foolish but it is a medium to your creative miracles.

Creative manifestation of the power of God is real!

Power over nature and physical forces

Today people have attributed so many evils to nature and by nature they meant God. God is not the author of any evil. It is not God that causes tornado, earthquake, flood and hurricane that destroy people's life and properties. It is unfortunate that even the insurance company calls them the acts of God. God had promised right from the time of Noah that he will not destroy the earth with water (flood) anymore and the rainbow which we see today is actually the sign of that covenant;

And God spake unto Noah, and to his sons with him, saying, And I, behold, I establish my covenant with you, and with your seed after you; And with every living creature that is with you, of the fowl, of the cattle, and of every beast of the earth with you; from all that go out of the ark, to every beast of the earth. And I will establish my covenant with you; neither shall all flesh be cut off any more by the waters of a flood; neither shall there anymore be a flood to destroy the earth. And God said, This is the token of the covenant which I make between me and you and every living creature that is with you, for perpetual generations: I do set my bow in the cloud, and it shall be for a token of a covenant between me and the earth. And it shall come to pass, when I bring a cloud over the earth, that the bow shall be seen in the cloud: And I will remember my covenant, which is between me and you and every living creature of all flesh; and the waters shall no more become a flood to destroy all flesh.

-Genesis 9:8-15

So, you can understand that it is not the desire of God to destroy the earth. The destruction we are facing today is due to the activities of the devil.

Believers have authority over all the works of Satan including his activities over nature.

Behold, I give unto you power (authority) to tread on serpents and scorpions, and over all the power of the enemy: and nothing shall by any means hurt you.

-Luke 10:19

Our authority is over all the powers of the enemy, including his power to cause earthquake and other natural disaster. Nothing is permitted to hurt us. This can only be possible if we are in command and if we truly posses (take and use) the power that He had given us.

Jesus demonstrated that we could have power over nature when he rebuked the storm.

And there arose a great storm of wind, and the waves beat into the ship, so that it was now full. And he was in the hinder part of the ship, asleep on a pillow: and they awake him, and say unto him, Master, carest thou not that we perish? And he arose, and rebuked the wind, and said unto the sea, Peace, be still. And the wind ceased, and there was a great calm.

—Mark 4:37-39

When I finished out of high school at 18, I joined some group of friends in rubber tapping business. I hired a rubber plantation several kilometres away from my hometown. I walked 5 hours daily and will have to climb a very big mountain on the way to get to my plantation. I did this rubber tapping to earn a living. The greatest challenge of the business is rainfall. It is always a problem if the rubbers do not solidify before the rain falls because everything will be washed away and we cannot tap rubber immediately after the rain, as the trees will be wet. I have observed that each time I work rain will fall and spoil the work and this is something I have walked several kilometres to do. I continue to suffer this challenge until one day I decided to pray against rain.

The cloud was pregnant with rain; people were running to their house because a torrential rain was about to fall. I was in my plantation and all the trees were seriously

175

shaking. I held one of my rubber plantations and I cried out to Jesus, asking him to stop the rain for a while till I finish my work and my rubber solidified. Immediately the cloud was clear and dry and the rain stayed.

Since that day controlling rain from falling whenever I need to do anything becomes a common anointing on me.

I married in August and people told me that it was a bad time because it was a raining season but I know that rain couldn't spoil my work. In my town they are evil people that claim to control rain. They draw rain to spoil people functions except you bribe them. I was told to go and pay money so that rain will not fall on my engagement day but I refused. I prayed and no rain fell during that period. Praise the Lord!

You can pray against tornados, earthquake, flood and hurricane that have been ravaging your town and that satanic plaque will stay away. The faith that stops rain can stop earthquake;

And Jesus said unto them, Because of your unbelief: for verily I say unto you, If ye have faith as a grain of mustard seed, ye shall say unto this mountain, Remove hence to yonder place; and it shall remove; and nothing shall be impossible unto you.

-Matthew 17:20

Power of evangelism

The Holy Spirit energises us to do evangelism. Anyone that is truly baptised with the Holy Spirit will be thirsty to preach the word of God. Today what we see is tongue talking people that are always ashamed of preaching the word of God. I believe that so many people in the church are baptised with something else, which is not of the Holy Ghost. I have heard demon-possessed

> **The power of the Holy Spirit is meant to testify of Jesus.**

177

people speak in tongue on several occasions especially during deliverance.

If what you got is the power of the Holy Spirit, why then are you not witnessing Christ. The power of the Holy Spirit is meant to testify of Jesus.

But when the Comforter is come, whom I will send unto you from the Father, even the Spirit of truth, which proceedeth from the Father, he shall testify of me:

-John 15:26

The power of evangelism was very evident in the life of the apostles after they got baptised in the Holy Spirit. The initial exploit following the baptism of the Holy Spirit was the preaching of Peter that attracts 3000 souls to the church. The apostle went everywhere preaching Christ. Philip went down to Samaria and he preached Christ unto them; *Then Philip went down to the city of Samaria, and preached Christ unto them.*

-Acts 8:5

Power to preach Christ Jesus is a major dimension of the Holy Spirit manifestation. The essence of power over satan, deadly things and sicknesses is for us to be able to preach the gospel of Jesus Christ. Miracle becomes automatic if one is committed to the preaching of the gospel of Christ Jesus. The church now struggle for the manifestation of God's power because Jesus Christ is no longer the centre of their message.

> **One of the acid tests for identifying true baptism of the Holy Spirit is the anointing and power for evangelism.**

One of the acid tests for identifying true baptism of the Holy Spirit is the anointing and power for evangelism. Those that are truly baptised in the Holy Spirit will not be ashamed or feel shy to evangelize. The Holy Spirit in us is the Spirit of boldness.

For God hath not given us the spirit of fear; but of power, and of love, and of a sound mind.

-2Timothy 1:7

Everyone that is truly baptised in the Holy Spirit will not be afraid or ashamed of the gospel of Christ. Such one will be filled with power, love and sound mind.

For I am not ashamed of the gospel of Christ: for it is the power of God unto salvation to everyone that believeth; to the Jew first, and also to the Greek.

-Roman 1:16

The gospel is actually the power. What does the power do? It brings salvation! How come you have the power and not the gospel? The two must go together. Understand that the word of God is the surest rescue that you can offer to anyone. It is the best assistance to give to anyone. The gospel of Jesus is the power of God unto salvation. If what usually manifest through you in the form of speaking in tongue is the Spirit of God (power of God), then you will lead people unto salvation by introducing Christ to them.

Power for revelation

You don't know a spiritual man or woman by mere quoting the word of God because the devil also knows the word of God;

Then the devil taketh him up into the holy city, and setteth him on a pinnacle of the temple, And saith unto him, If thou be the Son of God, cast thyself down: for it is written, He shall give his angels charge concerning thee: and in their hands they shall bear thee up, lest at any time thou dash thy foot against a stone.

-Mathew 4:5-6

The devil can take someone up and set him or her at the pinnacle of the temple. It is not everyone in the temple that is born again. The devil today sends his messengers to the church. This people speak the word of God too. They are familiar with biblical terminology than some true belivers; *And no marvel; for Satan himself is transformed into an angel of light.*

- 2 Corinthians 11:14

Satan can transform himself into an angel of light, note that the bible did not say like an angel of light but into an angel of light. The devil can actually appear as angel of light. What will you do if the devil appears to you as an angel of light? Are you going to recognise him as satan or take him to be the angel of light? What will you do if the devil brings the word of God into your spirit? How will you know?

The only way we can recognise and destroy the plan of the devil is through revelation. I have long stop preaching the mere word of God, I preach the revelation that is in the word of God. Every child of God that operates in revelation has gotten an advantage over the devil because revelation is one of the things we have as the children of God, which the devil don't have.

Satan might know the word of God but he does not have access to the revelation that is in the word of God.

The time for judging this world has come, when Satan, the ruler of this world, will be cast out.

John 12:31 (NLT)

6. Yet when I am among mature believers, I do speak with words of wisdom, but not the kind of wisdom that belongs to this world or to the rulers of this world, who are soon forgotten. 7. No, the wisdom we speak of is the mystery of God—his plan that was previously hidden, even though he made it for our ultimate glory before the world began. 8. ***But the rulers of this world have not understood it; if they had, they would not have crucified our glorious Lord.***

-1 Corinthians 2:6-8 (NLT) *(bolden, mine)*

If you put the two scriptures above together, you will quickly understand that satan is the ruler (prince) of this world. ***But the rulers of this world have not understood it; if they had, they would not have crucified our glorious Lord,*** So you can see that satan lacks understanding (revelation). King James Version of the bible put it this way: *'for had they known it, they would not have crucified the Lord of glory' (verse 8).* Satan has no access to revelation of God but you do and that is a major advantage that you have over the devil.

Verse 6 said mature believers speak with words of wisdom (revelation), which the devil cannot understand.

With revelation you can easily know all the wiles of the enemy.

Without revelation you remain ignorant and satan will take advantage of you;

Lest Satan should get an advantage of us: for we are not ignorant of his devices

-2 Corinthians 2:11

Satan is thief. He is an advantage taker. You are poor because satan stole your money, you are childless because satan stole your children, you are hated because satan stole your favour, you are frustrated because satan stole your blessings. As you become aware of your privileges and right through the revelational knowledge of God you will begin to take back what belongs to you

Note that revelation comes through knowledge and knowledge is never a gift, it is something that you search

184

for. The more you search for the knowledge of God, the more of His revelation you will have.

Power for revelation is also a dimension of the power of the Holy Spirit. There are various ways that the Holy Spirit can reveal himself to anyone. It could be through dream, vision, reading and meditating on the bible, reading of anointed books as you are doing, it could be through friends, through preachers, the voice of your parent, hearing the voice of God directly and also through angelic visit. The list cannot be exhausted.

But how can you be sure if you are having the revelation of God or from God?

30 And it came to pass, as he sat at meat with them, he took bread, and blessed it, and brake, and gave to them. 31 And their eyes were opened, and they knew him; and he vanished out of their sight. 32. And they said one to another; Did not our heart burn within us, while he talked with us by the way, and while he opened to us the scriptures?

-Luke 24:30-32

185

The scripture above was the revelation of Jesus Christ after His resurrection to two of His disciples who were on a 7 miles journey to Emmaus. Jesus appeared to them on the way but they did not realize it was Jesus until He took bread, break it and gave it to them then their eyes was opened. That was the power of communion.

Isn't it amazingly painful that some of the most striking revelations that we have often initially pass unnoticed? If you had known that that prophet is the man God has set over your life you wouldn't have been wandering here and there, if you had known that he or she was your husband or wife you wouldn't have suffered delay till date, if you have known the course to read, business to do and where to reside, your life would have been changed for the better by now. Communion with God is what gives and keeps your revelation alive

There was something very striking when they had the revelation of Jesus Christ in verse 32; the bible recorded that their hearts were burning within them, in other word there were greatly moved and motivated within them, they were filled with revival, there was a burning of the

Holy Spirit within them while he both talked with them and teach them the scripture.

Your Spirit will be revived each time you talked with an anointed man of God. Your heart will always burn within you each time an anointed man of God is teaching and that differentiate ordinary teaching from revelational teaching.

With revelation comes revival. You can always tell whenever you are receiving revelation from God with the revival, joy and motivation that comes with it into your spirit. You will immediately know within yourself that this is a revelation and not doctrine. The devil might have access to your doctrine and speak to you through the doctrine dogma but he can never have access to revelation.

As from this hour you will begin to operate in the revelational dimension of the power of the Holy Spirit in Jesus name.

And the LORD appeared unto him in the plains of Mamre: and he sat in the tent door in the heat of the day; And he lift up his eyes and looked, and, lo, three men stood by him: and when he saw them, he ran to meet them from the tent door, and bowed himself toward the ground, And said, My Lord, if now I have found favour in thy sight, pass not away, I pray thee, from thy servant: Let a little water, I pray you, be fetched, and wash your feet, and rest yourselves under the tree: And I will fetch a morsel of bread, and comfort ye your hearts; after that ye shall pass on: for therefore are ye come to your servant. And they said, So do, as thou hast said. And Abraham hastened into the tent unto Sarah, and said, Make ready quickly three measures of fine meal, knead it, and make cakes upon the hearth. And Abraham ran unto the herd, and fetcht a calf tender and good, and gave it unto a young man; and he hasted to dress it. And he took butter, and milk, and the calf which he had dressed, and set it before them; and he stood by them under the tree, and they did eat. And they said unto him, Where is Sarah thy wife? And he said, Behold, in the tent. And he said, I will certainly return unto thee according to the time of life; and, lo, Sarah thy wife shall have a son. And Sarah heard it in the tent door, which was behind him. Now Abraham and Sarah were old and well stricken in age; and it ceased to be with Sarah after the manner of women.............

And the men rose up from thence, and looked toward Sodom: and Abraham went with them to bring them on the way. And the LORD said, Shall I hide from Abraham that thing which I do; Seeing that Abraham shall surely become a great and mighty nation, and all the nations of the earth shall be blessed in him? For I know him, that he will command his children and his household after him, and they shall keep the way of the LORD, to do justice and judgment; that the LORD may bring upon Abraham that which he hath spoken of him. And the LORD said, Because the cry of Sodom and Gomorrah is great, and because their sin is very grievous...

And Abraham drew near, and said, Wilt thou also destroy the righteous with the wicked? Peradventure there be fifty righteous within the city: wilt thou also destroy and not spare the place for the fifty righteous that are therein? That be far from thee to do after this manner, to slay the righteous with the wicked: and that the righteous should be as the wicked, that be far from thee: Shall not the Judge of all the earth do right? And the LORD said, If I find in Sodom fifty righteous within the city, then I will spare all the place for their sakes. And Abraham answered and said, Behold now, I have taken upon me to speak unto the Lord, which am but dust and ashes: Peradventure there shall lack five of the fifty righteous: wilt thou destroy all the city for lack of five? And he said, If I find there forty and five, I will not destroy it. And he spake unto him yet again, and said, Peradventure there shall be forty found there. And he said, I will not do it for forty's sake. And he said unto him, Oh let not the Lord be angry, and I will speak: Peradventure there shall thirty be found there. And he said, I will not do it, if I find thirty there. And he said, Behold now, I have taken upon me to speak unto the Lord: Peradventure there shall be twenty found there. And he said, I will not destroy it for twenty's sake. And he said, Oh let not the Lord be angry, and I will speak yet but this once: Peradventure ten shall be found there. And he said, I will not destroy it for ten's sake. And the LORD went his way, as soon as he had left communing with Abraham: and Abraham returned unto his place

-Genesis18: 1-11, 16-20, 23-33

And Abraham gat up early in the morning to the place where he stood before the LORD: And he looked toward Sodom and Gomorrah, and toward all the land of the plain, and beheld, and, lo, the smoke of the country went up as the smoke of a furnace. And it came to pass, when God destroyed the cities of the plain, that God remembered Abraham, and sent Lot out of the midst of the overthrow, when he overthrew the cities in the which Lot dwelt.

-Genesis19:27-29.

There are certain things you can do to activate the revelational power of the Holy Spirit.

Nothing activates the power for revelation as sacrifice. Abraham compelled the three men to come for refreshment. He wanted to empty his entire house for these angels of God in the form of men. He offered them water, cake, fine good calf, butter and milk. He opened the angel's mouth through the power of sacrifice and they began to ask for Serah to bless her. They indeed bless the house of Abraham by proclaiming to their life that God will give them a man-child according to the time of life.

> **There are times that you have to sacrifice your way to revelations and prosperity. Sacrifice is another spiritual force that opens divine doors.**

Abraham took advantage of the opportunity to make supplication for Sodom and Gomorrah. His prayer brought deliverance for lot and his household.

There are times that you have to sacrifice your way to revelations and prosperity. Sacrifice is another spiritual force that opens divine door.

And Solomon went up thither to the brasen altar before the LORD, which was at the tabernacle of the congregation, and offered a thousand burnt offerings upon it. In that night did God appear unto Solomon, and said unto him, Ask what I shall give thee. And Solomon said unto God, Thou hast shewed great mercy unto David my father, and hast made me to reign in his stead.

-2Chronicles1:6-8

The Lord appeared unto Solomon the very night that he offered a burnt offering giving him an open cheque. **It is not said to be sacrifice until you give something costly and valuable to God.** Sacrifice opens you up to divine revelation and divine revelation guarantees your divine blessing.

It is not said to be sacrifice until you give something costly and valuable to God. David said I will not give to God that which cost me nothing.

And the king said unto Araunah, Nay; but I will surely buy it of thee at a price: neither will I offer burnt offerings unto the LORD my God of that which doth cost me nothing. So David bought the threshing floor and the oxen for fifty shekels of silver.

-2Samuel 24:24

Sacrifice is different from offering; sacrifice is giving to God that thing which you think is so dare to you. The value and degree of the revelation and blessing that you receive is determined by the cost of your sacrifice.

And when he looked on him, he was afraid, and said, What is it, Lord? And he said unto him, Thy prayers and thine alms are come up for a memorial before God. And now send men to Joppa, and call for one Simon, whose surname is Peter: He lodgeth with one Simon a tanner, whose house is by the sea side: he shall tell thee what thou oughtest to do............. Then Peter opened his mouth, and said, Of a truth I perceive that God is no respecter of persons: But in every nation he that feareth him, and worketh righteousness, is accepted with him...........While Peter yet spake these words, the Holy Ghost fell on all them which heard the word. And they of the circumcision which believed were astonished, as many as came with Peter, because that on the Gentiles also was poured out the gift of the Holy Ghost.

- Acts 10:4-6, 34-36, and 44-45.

Sacrifice can work out divine revelation. Your sacrifice can give you divine connection too. God differently spoke to Cornelius and Peter at the same time. Your sacrifice can make something unusual happen for your good. Sacrifice can open the door of that which you think is impossible.

> I believe that God is about to change protocol for your favour.

Note that at this time there was a strong racism even in the church that the Jews has no dealing with the Gentiles but the power of God moved Peter to go and minister to Cornelius. God has to change protocol about the norms of the Jew in a revelation to Peter just to compel him to go and minister to Cornelius. I believe that God is about to change protocol for your favour.

Both the revelation of peter and Cornelius is motivated by the power of the Holy Spirit

Another thing that motivates revelation is the word of God. His word can come either through the scripture, listening to anointed men of God or reading of anointed books.

And the LORD appeared again in Shiloh: for the LORD revealed himself to Samuel in Shiloh by the word of the LORD.

-1Samuel 3:21

One of the usual ways that God appear to people is by the word of God. God also uses his word to confirm revelations. God revealed himself to Samuel in Shiloh by the word of God. He has not changed therefore he is still revealing himself to people today through His word.

It is therefore very important to study and meditate on the word of God. Meditation on the word of God translates one into the presence of God.

This book of the law shall not depart out of thy mouth; but thou shalt meditate therein day and night, that thou mayest observe to do according to all that is written therein: for then thou shalt make thy way prosperous, and then thou shalt have good success.

-Joshua 1:8

Before you can meditate on the word of God, you first must have the word close to you. *This book of the law and* not *that book of the law,* meaning that the word must be very close to you first. Secondly, you have to read the word of God, that is, putting it in your mouth and to keep saying it. Thirdly, you must meditate on the word. The word meditation means to mutter or utter quietly while thinking on it. To me a good synonym to mediation is ruminating, which actually mean to think deeply about something. It means to 'chew the chord'. Goats or other ruminant animals chew their chord and are termed as ruminant animals. They will chew and swallow the grass severally. The first swallow goes to the first compartment of their stomach (the rumen), they will again regurgitate it back into the mouth when the need arises and chew it again which then goes into the second compartment of their stomach (the reticulum). The process continues until the food (grass) gets to the omasum (3rd compartment) and abomasum (4th compartment) respectively. This is exactly what we need to do with the word. This is indeed meditation!

The word of God needs to be properly digested into your spirit man so that you can extract all the nutrients therein. You need to keep meditating on the word for this proper digestion to take place. Keep it within you and once in a while regurgitate the word by muttering it while thinking deeply about it (meditation).

Thy words were found, and I did eat them; and thy word was unto me the joy and rejoicing of mine heart: for I am called by thy name, O LORD God of hosts.

Jeremiah 15:16

The word of God can be eaten just like what ruminant animals do with grasses. No one will see delicious food and not be happy. The word indeed brings joy to the heart and with joy comes salvation;

Therefore with joy shall ye draw water out of the wells of salvation.

Isaiah 12:3

With the word comes joy and with joy come salvation because joy is the hand that can draw from the abundance (well) of the saving power of God. That is why the bible said if we meditate on the word of God we would have good success. Good success is the product of a happy and joyful heart.

> **Good success comes through the word of God alone. Prostitution and cheating do not give good success.**

Good success comes through the word of God alone. Prostitution and cheating do not give good success. The only medium that one can achieve good success is through the word of God because the word of God helps you to gain access to revelation. For good success to be

> **Everything is at the command of the word of God because the word of God created everything.**

delivered you must make the word of God your food. It must not depart from your mouth. You got to keep saying it, you got to keep meditating on it day and night.

Everything is at the command of the word of God because the word of God created everything. The word of God is the medium through which the Holy Spirit can communicate with you. Meditating on the word of God gives the Holy Spirit access to lunch you into the realm of revelation. It is good to create a quite time for you to meditate on the word of God. A night vigil on the word of God is worth having.

I John, who also am your brother, and companion in tribulation, and in the kingdom and patience of Jesus Christ, was in the isle that is called Patmos, for the word of God, and for the testimony of Jesus Christ. I was in the Spirit on the Lord's day, and heard behind me a great voice, as of a trumpet, Saying, I am Alpha and Omega, the first and the last: and, What thou seest, write in a book, and send it unto the seven churches which are in Asia; unto Ephesus, and unto Smyrna, and unto Pergamos, and unto Thyatira, and unto Sardis, and unto Philadelphia, and unto Laodicea.

-Revelation 1:9-11

John was thrown into the isle of Patmos for the sake of the word of God. He was still meditating on the word of God as the bible recorded that he was in the Spirit on the Lord's Day which also implies that he was still observing his regular worship with Jesus and he heard the word of God so loud and clear.

One wonderful thing about the word of God is that while we are reading the word, we are also hearing the word. The word we are reading is called the '*logos*' (the written word), while the one we are hearing is called the '*rhema*' (the spoken word). It is the '*rhema*' that produces faith. Faith can only come when '*rhema*' come.

So then faith cometh by hearing, and hearing by the word of God. -Romans 10:17

Faith does not come by preaching or reading the word of God; faith comes by hearing the word of God, which means hearing from God, the '*rhema*'.

The voice of God will be so clear to you if you can lunch into the realm of the Spirit. John wrote letters that still describe the state of the church today because he had fellowship with the Spirit of God. It is a timeless letter of warning to the church of God.

The Holy Spirit empowers us into the realm of revelation as we give him time to the study of the word of God.

People ask how I do hear from God. The secret lies in developing relationship with God and in studying and meditating on His word. I will not talk much on this as I advice that you read the book I wrote on how to hear from God.

I lost my dear elder brother in November 9, 2003 to accident. It was so painful that I began to pray and fast. I fasted for 70 days and the Lord told me that they was an idol that was buried at the foundation of my father's house that has been causing untimely death in the family. The plaque stopped when the idol was removed.

When you are empowered revelation is the outcome.

Anyone that cannot hear the voice of God has no future. Only God can show you the future, only God can show you a husband/wife whose wealth will last, only God can know a husband/wife that though look good today will break down with insanity tomorrow, only God can show a business man not to buy or invest in business that have no future. Indeed, it is only God that can show you your destiny. You will do well once you get to both know and do what God has created you for.

> **Anyone that cannot hear the voice of God has no future.**

Note that John was in the Spirit before he was able to gain access to the realm of revelation. God is a Spirit and before you can hear from him you got to lunch into the realm of the Spirit. Revelation is one of the dimensions of the Holy Spirit power.

Words empowerment

Words can only be fulfils if they are empowered by the power of the Holy Spirit. The Holy Spirit was incubating on the earth before the word of God came to fulfilment.

And the earth was without form, and void; and darkness was upon the face of the deep. And the Spirit of God moved upon the face of the waters. And God said, Let there be light: and there was light

.-Genesis 1:2-3

Even God did not speak until the Holy Spirit moved. Make sure you only speak or prophesy when the Holy Spirit moves.

If the word of God needed to be empowered and incubated upon by the Holy Spirit before fulfilment let alone the words of man. It is the responsibility of the Holy Spirit to empower our words to fulfilment.

For thus saith the LORD God of Israel, The barrel of meal shall not waste, neither shall the cruse of oil fail, until the day that the LORD sendeth rain upon the earth.......And the barrel of meal wasted not, neither did the cruse of oil fail, according to the word of the LORD, which he spake by Elijah.

-1 King 17:14-16

Those that are truly empowered by the Holy Spirit see whatever they say. Your word begins to have weight once the fire of the Holy Spirit has sanctified your tongue.

Then said I, Woe is me! for I am undone; because I am a man of unclean lips, and I dwell in the midst of a people of unclean lips: for mine eyes have seen the King, the LORD of hosts. Then flew one of the seraphims unto me, having a live coal in his hand, which he had taken with the tongs from off the altar: And he laid it upon my mouth, and said, Lo, this hath touched thy lips; and thine iniquity is taken away, and thy sin purged. Also I heard the voice of the Lord, saying, Whom shall I send, and who will go for us? Then said I, Here am I; send me.

-Isaiah 6:5-8

Your tongue has have to be sanctified with the fire of the Holy Spirit Before your mouth can be used as God's tool in declaring his words and in commanding blessing. There is a fire at the altar of heaven that can sanctify your tongue before your words can become potent. The reason Peter's message was so powerful on the day of Pentecost was because of the divided tongue of fire. It is with this divided tongue of fire that Philip was able to preach Jesus in the city of Samaria.

Divided tongue of fire means that part of their tongue has been translated by the power of the Holy Spirit. It means a divine touch on their tongue, a divine link that enables them to declare and prophesy according to the dictates of heaven.

Then there appeared to them divided tongues, as of fire, and one sat upon each of them. And they were all filled with the Holy Spirit and began to speak with other tongues, as the Spirit gave them utterance

- Acts 2:3-4.(NKJV)

When the power of the Holy Spirit comes upon you it translates your tongue and when your tongue is translated your words will be empowered and when your words are empowered whatever you said come to fulfilment.

CHAPTER FIVE

THE PRICE FOR POWER

The value of a thing is determined from the cost of it. Everyone likes enjoyment but not everyone will like to pay the price. Anointing (power) is beautiful if you can pay the price. Our generation need the power of God and God is looking for people that He can pour the anointing upon.

I will like to emphasize again that the anointing or power dimension of the Holy Spirit is different from the baptism of the Holy Spirit, which is why people that are all baptised in the Holy Spirit do not all have the same anointing.

> **...people that are all baptised in the Holy Spirit do not all have the same anointing.**

But ye shall receive power (anointing), after that the Holy Ghost is come upon you: and ye shall be witnesses unto me both in Jerusalem, and in all Judaea, and in Samaria, and unto the uttermost part of the earth.

-Acts 1:8

Power (anointing) comes **after** that the Holy Spirit is come upon you, which means that after receiving the Holy Spirit you need to activate His power within you. Just as one can get a book without knowing what is inside except you read it that is how you will not be able to get the fullness of the Holy Spirit unless you activate it. The baptism of the Holy Spirit is one thing and operating in the full power (anointing) dimension of Holy Spirit is another thing.

How God anointed Jesus of Nazareth with the Holy Ghost and with power: who went about doing good, and healing all that were oppressed of the devil; for God was with him.

-Acts 10:38

209

The phrase *'with the Holy Ghost and with power'* reveals another power (anointing) dimension form mere receiving of the Holy Ghost. There is the receiving of the Holy Ghost and there is a special power (anointing) that follows after receiving the Holy Ghost.

The manifestation of the power of God is in dimension. The price you pay and your level of holiness and consecration determine the level of operation.

Afterward he brought me again unto the door of the house; and, behold, waters issued out from under the threshold of the house eastward: for the forefront of the house stood toward the east, and the waters came down from under from the right side of the house, at the south side of the altar. Then brought he me out of the way of the gate northward, and led me about the way without unto the utter gate by the way that looketh eastward; and, behold, there ran out waters on the right side. And when the man that had the line in his hand went forth eastward, he measured a thousand cubits, and he brought me through the waters; the waters were to the ankles. Again he measured a thousand, and brought me through the waters; the waters were to the knees. Again he measured a thousand, and brought me through; the waters were to the loins. Afterward he measured a thousand; and it was a river that I could not pass over: for the waters were risen, waters to swim in, a river that could not be passed over.

-Ezekiel 47:1-5

The water here signifies the anointing of the Holy Spirit. The scripture above pictured levels of anointing; there is an ankle, knee, loin and the overflowing levels of the power of God. The level attained depends on how far you go. Each level differ from the next by a thousand cubits meaning that the more you can go in rubbing your spirit with that of God the more of God's power at work in you. The difference in anointing among believers is actually in thousands. Very clear difference exists among us in terms of the power we command even thou we are all baptized in the Holy Spirit.

Every anointing of the Holy Spirit is not without price. I was plagued some time ago with Asthma and sudden weakness. Breathing was so difficult for me. After some days I began to ask God to show me the secret of divine healing and supernatural manifestation of his power. The answer I got was a surprise. God told me that He does not bestow His power anyhow and that those that have access to His power are those that have intimate relationship with Him. In that revelation I saw that people in the kingdom of God are in different levels, even though every one of them was born again.

I saw a fenced building, some people were within the fence, other were inside of the building in the sitting room, others were in the bedroom while others were lying at the chest of Jesus and I heard a voice saying; 'those lying on the chest of Jesus are those that have access to the supernatural manifestation of the power of God'. When I woke up I know that there are price to pay before one can manifest the supernatural power of God.

Power cannot just come so cheaply, if it come that way you will think you made it by your own strength and you might abuse it but if you labour for it you will guide it jealously, that could probably be the reason God will have us pay the price before we can receive it.

When Elisha asked for the double portion of the Spirit of Elijah, he replied Elisha that he was asking for a *hard thing.*

And he said, Thou hast asked a hard thing: nevertheless, if thou see me when I am taken from thee, it shall be so unto thee; but if not, it shall not be so.

-2Kings 2:10

This shows that power is not cheap and do not just come. The church today is not experiencing the fullness of Christ's power because they are not ready to pay the prices. Elijah said that it is a hard thing but if Elisha can be focused on him when he will be taken to heaven, then he can have the double potion of his anointing. This prophet of fire was taken to heaven in a chariot of fire and whirl wind. It takes a serious and focused spirit to see someone in the chariot of fire surrounded by whirlwind.

PERSISTENT FOCUSED PRAYER

Elisha

And it came to pass, when the LORD would take up Elijah into heaven by a whirlwind that Elijah went with Elisha from Gilgal. And Elijah said unto Elisha, Tarry here, I pray thee; for the LORD hath sent me to Bethel. And Elisha said unto him, As the LORD liveth, and as thy soul liveth, I will not leave thee. So they went down to Bethel.

And the sons of the prophets that were at Bethel came forth to Elisha, and said unto him, Knowest thou that the LORD will take away thy master from thy head today? And he said, Yea, I know it; hold ye your peace. And Elijah said unto him, Elisha, tarry here, I pray thee; for the LORD hath sent me to Jericho. And he said, As the LORD liveth, and as thy soul liveth, I will not leave thee. So they came to Jericho.

And the sons of the prophets that were at Jericho came to Elisha, and said unto him, Knowest thou that the LORD will take away thy master from thy head today?

And he answered, Yea, I know it; hold ye your peace. And Elijah said unto him, Tarry, I pray thee, here; for the LORD hath sent me to Jordan. And he said, As the LORD liveth, and as thy soul liveth, I will not leave thee. And they two went on.

And fifty men of the sons of the prophets went, and stood to view afar off: and they two stood by Jordan. And Elijah took his mantle, and wrapped it together, and smote the waters, and they were divided hither and thither, so that they two went over on dry ground. And it came to pass, when they were gone over, that Elijah said unto Elisha, Ask what I shall do for thee, before I be taken away from thee. And Elisha said, I pray thee, let a double portion of thy spirit be upon me. And he said, Thou hast asked a hard thing: nevertheless, if thou see me when I am taken from thee, it shall be so unto thee; but if not, it shall not be so.

And it came to pass, as they still went on, and talked, that, behold, there appeared a chariot of fire, and horses of fire, and parted them both asunder; and Elijah went up by a whirlwind into heaven. And Elisha saw it, and he cried, My father, my father, the chariot of Israel, and the horsemen thereof. And he saw him no more: and he took hold of his own clothes, and rent them in two pieces. He took up also the mantle of Elijah that fell from him, and went back, and stood by the bank of Jordan; And he took the mantle of Elijah that fell from him, and smote the waters, and said, Where is the LORD God of Elijah? and when he also had smitten the waters, they parted hither and thither: and Elisha went over.

-2 King 2:1-14

Can you see the degree of distraction that Elisha encounters in his search for power? Elijah said to him tarry here for the Lord has sent me to Bethel but Elisha will never give up. The sons of the prophets in Bethel also gathered and persuade Elisha that he should not waste his time that the Lord will take away his

> **When people cannot convince you they becomes spectators to see how you will end, expecting your down fall.**

master from him today, yet Elisha will not give up. When they got to Jericho Elijah repeated the same thing

> **When you get result those that are trying to distract you will become your affiliates.**

and likewise the sons of the prophet but he still cannot give up and the same incidence happened the third time in Jordan but Elisha still could not give up. The bible recorded as read above that the sons of the prophets gathered together afar off and began to look to see what will happen to this prophet Elisha that refused to listen to their prophecy.

When people cannot convince you they becomes spectators to see how you will end, expecting your down fall. But Elisha was persistent and he got result. *The only way you can shame your enemy is to get result.*

You sometimes know the value of something through the level of distraction that you receive. It is unfortunate that a lot of people give up with distraction when distraction actually means persistence. It will take the revelation of the Holy Spirit to know that distraction means

217

persistence. Sometimes this distraction may seem to come from even God himself, why? Probably because He will want to know 'how bad' you need it.

It looked as if Elijah has planned with the sons of the prophets to discourage Elisha but it was not so. Remember that Elijah was a man of God, also the sons of the prophets were prophesying rightly but Elisha will not be carried away by their prophecy, he was desperate to receive the power from Elijah.

That you have to stretch and stress yourself to get it does not mean that it doesn't belong to you.

If it were we today we would have quickly quoted the scripture that says in the mouth of 2 or 3 witness every matter is established and probably would have given up. We would have even thought that these prophecies are getting too much and probably it is not the will of God to seek for the power any further.

Persistent focused prayer works and that was what changed the destiny of Jacob.

Jacob

And Jacob was left alone; and there wrestled a man with him until the breaking of the day. And when he saw that he prevailed not against him, he touched the hollow of his thigh; and the hollow of Jacob's thigh was out of joint, as he wrestled with him. And he said, Let me go, for the day breaketh. And he said, I will not let thee go, except thou bless me. And he said unto him, What is thy name? And he said, Jacob. And he said, Thy name shall be called no more Jacob, but Israel: for as a prince hast thou power with God and with men, and hast prevailed. And Jacob asked him, and said, Tell me, I pray thee, thy name. And he said, Wherefore is it that thou dost ask after my name?

And he blessed him there. And Jacob called the name of the place Peniel: for I have seen God face to face, and my life is preserved.

—Genesis 32:24-30

Here again we see Jacob wrestling with an angel alone. Most people that truly had the impact of the Spirit upon their lives mostly received such anointing on the private alter of prayer. Church service is good but it is not an environment for you to really wrestle with an angel. The dimension of persistent focused prayer that lunch one into the overflowing anointing of the Holy Spirit is called wrestling; it connotes a serious focused battle.

> **Everyone that truly had the impact of the Spirit upon his/her life mostly received such anointing on the private alter of prayer.**

Personal private alter of prayer is an effective avenue where you can wrestle with God. When the angel saw the determination of Jacob he asked for his name. It is an indication therefore that the meaning of his name had been responsible for his challenges. Jacob means supplanter or deceiver.

When you wrestle with God, He touches you at the point of your need to deliver your blessing.

Note that Jacob did not only have his name changed as many people thought, he was blessed with all kinds of blessings by the angel

But why must Jacob wrestle with an angel till the breaking forth of the day? Why will the angel allow such a long period of engagement in warfare? If it is to be you, may be you would have given up. Discouragement sometimes is an index to great dimension of blessing. You can tell or evaluate the dimension of your blessing by the level of discouragement that you receive. Discouragement actually should mean that you should be persistent. Discouragement is a blessing sensor; it usually senses your coming blessing and tries to stop it.

Discourageme nt sometimes is an index to great dimension of blessing

I use to be persistent ever since the Holy Spirit gave me this revelation. Don't always give up in the face of discouragement.

221

No good treasures of the earth are found at the surface. Gold are buried in the heart of the earth, crude oil are either buried in the heart of the earth or sea. It takes a very serious effort to get them out. *The cost of mining them is almost as if you sell all your belongings to have them out, such also is the power and the kingdom of God.*

Again, the kingdom of heaven is like unto treasure hid in a field; the which when a man hath found, he hideth, and for joy thereof goeth and selleth all that he hath, and buyeth that field. Again, the kingdom of heaven is like unto a merchant man, seeking goodly pearls: Who, when he had found one pearl of great price, went and sold all that he had, and bought it.

-Mathew 13:44-46

Understand that it might cost you so many things such as certificate, time and money to gain access to the power of God.

The kingdom of God is a goodly pearl that is of a great price.

Note that the kingdom of God is synonymous to the power of God;

But if I with the finger of God cast out devils, no doubt the kingdom of God is come upon you.

-Luke 11:20

The Kingdom of God is also a state of command and a state of operation in absolute power.

You begin to live the kingdom kind of life when you begin to exercise authority over the devil and all his works.

Jacob wrestle with an angel and when he saw that Jacob was determined not to let him go, he touched the hollow of his thigh and it was dislocated. Have you ever prayed until your legs were

> **When you have power with God you will demonstrate that power with men.**

223

out of joint? I do pray until my legs are 'frozen' due to posture, sometimes my hands and some time excruciating pain at my chest region but not to the extent of suffering dislocation. So, you can understand the dimension of wrestling that Jacob had here.

The prayer of Jacob is a prevailing one. The angel in his own language said 'you got power with God and with men'. When you have power with God you will demonstrate that power with men. But you got to pay the price to acquire power with God.

Elijah

And Elijah said unto Ahab, Get thee up, eat and drink; for there is a sound of abundance of rain. So Ahab went up to eat and to drink. And Elijah went up to the top of Carmel; and he cast himself down upon the earth, and put his face between his knees, And said to his servant, Go up now, look toward the sea. And he went up, and looked, and said, There is nothing. And he said, Go again seven times. And it came to pass at the seventh time, that he said, Behold, there ariseth a little cloud out of the sea, like a man's hand. And he said, Go up, say unto Ahab, Prepare thy chariot, and get thee down, that the rain stop thee not. And it came to pass in the mean while, that the heaven was black with clouds and wind, and there was a great rain. And Ahab rode, and went to Jezreel.

-1 King 18:41-45

Elijah was a man that was committed to persistent prayer. Every move of God is born out of fierce consistent prayer.

> **Every move of God is born out of fierce consistent prayer.**

There was a lady in my office in those days that has almost past the flower of her age without a husband, she realized the cost of power and began to pray. She gave thanks to God for her husband 8000 times and her husband showed up. These single stretch of thanksgiving prayer cost her about a 24 hours of prayer on her knees.

I have seen a woman of about 68 years who was married for thirty something years gave birth to a baby boy after engaging in 21 days of prayer warfare at mid nights.

When I graduated, though with first class, I have to engage in serious prayer warfare and sacrifice for my job to show up. I sang an anointed song for 12 hours at a stretch while folding myself on my knee at a corner of my single room. It cost me entire day warfare and my destiny changed till today. After that moment, I touch money as people touch sand. You may jealous people that God has blessed not knowing the price they had paid.

Every move of God is born out of fierce consistent prayer and Elijah understood that principle. He prophesied that there will be sounds of abundance of rain and the king went for joy but he went to the top of the mountain to pray. He cast himself down and put his face between his knees. That was a serious prayer warfare moment.

One might ask; must he cast himself down and suffer his body for the Lord to hear his prayer, must he go to the mountain for his prayer to be heard? You need to understand that Elijah did not cast himself

You only stop praying when you get your desires delivered. People that knows the value of what they need fights discouragement.

down for self pity neither did he cast himself down to receive sympathy from God but sometimes, there is a way a desire will be too strong in your heart that you cannot but to cast yourself down.

What made me to fold myself and pray intensively is not self-pity or just emotion but the strong desire boiling within me caused it. If you have a very strong and desperate desire to see the move of God in your life, family, business, and ministry and in the world you will not know when to do the same. Elijah was a man with a mountain top experience, he prayed until he got result. He asked his servant to keep checking the cloud until there is a sign of rain and he went seven times. You only stop praying when you get your desires delivered. People that knows the value of what they need fights discouragement.

Jairus: (The leader of the synagogue)

And, behold, there cometh one of the rulers of the synagogue, Jairus by name; and when he saw him, he fell at his feet, And besought him greatly, saying, My little daughter lieth at the point of death: I pray thee, come and lay thy hands on her, that she may be healed; and she shall live..........

While he yet spake, there came from the ruler of the synagogue's house certain which said, Thy ....daughter is dead: why troublest thou the Master any further? As soon as Jesus heard the word that was spoken, he saith unto the ruler of the synagogue, Be not afraid, only believe. And he suffered no man to follow him, save Peter, and James, and John the brother of James And he cometh to the house of the ruler of the synagogue, and seeth the tumult, and them that wept and wailed greatly. And when he was come in, he saith unto them, Why make ye this ado, and weep? the damsel is not dead, but sleepeth. And they laughed him to scorn. But when he had put them all out, he taketh the father and the mother of the damsel, and them that were with him, and entereth in where the damsel was lying. And he took the damsel by the hand, and said unto her, Talitha cumi; which is, being interpreted, Damsel, I say unto thee, arise. And straightway the damsel arose, and walked; for she was of the age of twelve years. And they were astonished with a great astonishment.

-Mark 5:22, 35-42

Jairus who was the leader of synagogue came to Jesus requesting that He should come and heal his 12 years old daughter that was sick.

I will like you to understand that this leader of the synagogue has been with Jesus all day even before the woman with the issue of blood came and he got no answer (verses 22-35 of Mark chapter 5). The man was

> **.....but when something bad happens volunteer messengers are just all over.**

with Jesus till messengers came from home that he should stop disturbing himself that the child was already dead.

Do you have messengers of satan telling you to forget about Jesus or this church thing? I have noticed that when someone has good news to give messengers don't easily come-by. When we need to preach the gospel messengers don't readily come-by but when something bad happens volunteer messengers are just all over.

Why had this man been with Jesus all day and got no answer? Could it be lack of faith? When Jesus overheard the messengers delivering that message of discouragement He whispers to him '*be not afraid. Only believe*' (KJV) which means do not be seized with the alarm and struck with fear, '*only keep on believing*' (AMP), meaning he got faith.

The reason for the 'delayed' answer is also not far from why Jacob has to wrestle with the angel all night, Elisha following Elijah in the face of discouragements and Elijah sending his servant seven times to keep on checking the cloud.

Jesus eventually responded and by that time Jairus daughter was already dead but death is just like a bend with God. Praise God He raised her up!

As I kept saying, that discouragement sometimes serves as a signal to the level of blessing about to be possessed. And one thing with discouragement is that it often comes from the direction you least expect, it mostly comes from the people you expect to be an encouragement to you.

Looking at the discouragement that Jacob, Elisha and Jairus faced, you will see that they seem to come from God. Does it mean that God discourage people? Do not be confused! God might try your faith or patience, which you might interpret as discouragement. One will always know the trial of faith or patience that seems to come from God by an inner force of persistence that drives you. See the evidence below;

For it is God which worketh in you both to will and to do of his good pleasure.

-Philippians 2:13

Though the angel seems not to answer Jacob as quickly as possible, though Elijah seems not to be encouraging to Elisha, though Jesus seems to be silent for a while to Jairus, yet God was working in them to continue with their desire and to be persistent. God will never allow you to be discouraged. The discouragement that made you to give up the other day is not from God. You will always know when God does His own things if you have spiritual understanding.

Distraction and discouragement such as sicknesses and diseases cannot be from God; He cannot tempt anyone with evil.

Just as I told people that the fire from God is always different from satanic fire. God's kind of fire attracts you to Him. The fire from God is to catch more of your attention. It will never consume you.

And the angel of the LORD appeared unto him in a flame of fire out of the midst of a bush: and he looked, and, beholds, the bush burned with fire, and the bush was not consumed. And Moses said, I will now turn aside, and see this great sight, why the bush is not burnt. And when the LORD saw that he turned aside to see, God called unto him out of the midst of the bush, and said, Moses, Moses. And he said, Here am I.

-Exodus 3:2-4

The bush burned with fire but it was not consumed. The fire of God might burn but it will not consume you. Jesus come that you might have life and has it more abundantly. It is only the fire that comes from satan that will burn to consume you. The fire of God strengthens and attracts you to him

> **The fire from God is to catch more of your attention it will not consume you.**

233

but the fire from Satan threatens and destroys you. *Satan is a thief!*

The thief cometh not, but for to steal, and to kill, and to destroy: I am come that they might have life, and that they might have it more abundantly.

-John 10:10

I see God working encouragement and determination in you until your needed blessing is delivered. Your expectation will never be cut off in Jesus name.

The hope of the righteous shall be gladness: but the expectation of the wicked shall perish.

-Proverb 10:28

The fear of the wicked, it shall come upon him: but the desire of the righteous shall be granted.

-Proverb 10:24

God will grant you your desire because He is going to create that persistent ability to pray in you, until you see your needed blessing in your hand.

234

Remember that even Jesus being the Son of God has to pray persistently and vigorously to be empowered before He can fulfil destiny even though his assignment was in line with heaven. You need empowerment like Jesus to be able to fulfil your destiny or your calling.

Jesus

Prayer was the lifestyle of Jesus. Let us consider His dimension of prayer.

And he withdrew himself into the wilderness, and prayed.

-Luke 5:16.

Have you ever been into the wilderness? Jesus withdrew Himself into the wilderness and prayed. I know that people do not live in the wilderness. The wilderness must have been sited far away from where people lived. Jesus is someone that creates time for prayer. Prayer was so important to Him that He creates time for it. Prayer is His priority. He always creates time to pray; consider the distance to the wilderness let alone the time spent on prayer.

One can tell what one place his/her value upon by the kind of attention he or she gives to something. *Jesus withdrew Himself far into the wilderness to be refuelled each time he impacts anointing, meaning that anointing can be depleted.*

Remember that Jesus was in all ramifications existing as a human being at this time. Some people might settle down for 'enjoyment' when they began to see results.

> **Results actually should mean more work and more work implies more result; that was the wisdom of Jesus.**

Jesus had both the wilderness and the mountain top experience of prayer. When you have the wilderness prayer experience you overcome dryness and when you have the mountain top prayer experience you overcome difficulties and challenges and that explains why none of the challenges could move Jesus.

236

And when he had sent the multitudes away, he went up into a mountain apart to pray: and when the evening was come, he was there alone

-Mathew 14:23.

You must create time to pray amidst your counselling tight schedule in order to avoid cancelling yourself out of ministry.

Crowd of blessing is good but sometimes make sure you are not carried away with it. There are times you need to close your shop and go to fellowship to be refreshed irrespective of the amount of customers that are coming.

I went to school in a core Islamic state and I noticed that those Muslims in the market would always close their shop whenever it is time for their prayer. Sometimes we seem to have left or sold out these principles to the devil.

You need to take break in the office for a prayer walk, there are times you need to close your textbooks for a prayer walk, and you got to cut down on the time you spend on watching television for prayer. You must create time to pray amidst your counselling tight schedule in order to avoid cancelling yourself out of ministry. Jesus sends the crowd away to have time for prayer.

You pay the price of power on the altar of prayer. It is a common and a true saying that a prayerless Christian is a powerless Christian. You say it but you don't do it! Thank God

> **Prayer indeed is the platform of power. When you earnestly and eagerly pray something will always happen.**

that you know that some Christians are powerless. Are you among them?

And being in an agony he prayed more earnestly: and his sweat was as it were great drops of blood falling down to the ground.

-Luke 22:44

Imagine! That Jesus so prayed and His sweats were as thick as '*clots of blood*' (AMP). He prayed earnestly because He was in agony of spirit. What is your agony and how do you handle it? Jesus chooses to pray than complain, what about you? The answer lies in prayer. Prayer indeed is the platform of power. When you earnestly and eagerly pray something will always happen.

Paul and Silas

And when they had laid many stripes upon them, they cast them into prison, charging the jailor to keep them safely: Who, having received such a charge, thrust them into the inner prison, and made their feet fast in the stocks. And at midnight Paul and Silas prayed, and sang praises unto God: and the prisoners heard them. And suddenly there was a great earthquake, so that the foundations of the prison were shaken: and immediately all the doors were opened, and every one's bands were loosed. And the keeper of the prison awaking out of his sleep, and seeing the prison doors open, he drew out his sword, and would have killed himself, supposing that the prisoners had been fled.

239

But Paul cried with a loud voice, saying, Do thyself no harm: for we are all here. Then he called for a light, and sprang in, and came trembling, and fell down before Paul and Silas, And brought them out, and said, Sirs, what must I do to be saved? And they said, Believe on the Lord Jesus Christ, and thou shalt be saved, and thy house.

-Acts 16:23-24

The devil does not respect your complain or self pity what the devil understand is the command of prayer

Those that know what to do don't panic. Paul and Silas knew what to do. They were arrested and put in prison for the sake of the gospel and at mid night they prayed and sang that everyone heard them.

Your own mid night could connote barrenness, financial difficulties, curses, stagnation and sicknesses and diseases. What do you do in your mid night?

The devil does not respect your complain or self pity what the devil understand is the command of prayer in

240

the name of Jesus. Nothing happens until you pray. Prayer catalyses the Spirit of power into action. *God will become an intruder if He intervenes in your situation without calling upon him. He will always ask the question; what will you like me to do for you?* Great and mighty things happen when we pray.

When Paul and Silas began to pray something happened;

'And suddenly there was a great earthquake, so that the foundations of the prison were shaken: and immediately all the doors were opened, and every one's bands were loosed'

This was a literal earthquake and not in the realm of the spirit. They were captured physically and not spiritually so, the power has to be demonstrated physically. The shakings that took place was so intense that the doors were opened and every band loosed.

When you pray deliverance answer in the realm that you need it. If you need deliverance in the physical it will happen literarily in the physical realm and if you need deliverance in the realm of the spirit it will happen in the

241

spiritual realm. I understand that certain bondage happens in the realm of the spiritual and translates into the realm of the physical, in such

> Sometimes you got to imagine your deliverance; if you cannot see it you cannot have it.

cases expect the fire of the Holy Spirit to burn from the spiritual to the physical.

I will like you to imagine the power that was released here when Paul and Silas prayed. As you imagine such deliverance it will begin to materialize in your life too in Jesus name.

You got to imagine your deliverance; if you cannot see it you cannot have it. Your imagination is very powerful. Imagination can turn to reality that is why the bible says we should constantly cast down imagination and every thought that raises itself above the knowledge of God. Positive imagination can become reality as much as negative imagination.

No one can stop a man or woman of prayer. They are people of exploit. Paul and Silas cannot be stopped even in the prison they were still winning soul because of the demonstration of God's power.

When power is in operation too much preaching is not needed. Mere demonstration of power alone will begin to convict men and women of their sins: like what happened to the keeper of the prison and to Peter that toiled all night before Jesus came to his rescue who immediately confessed that he was a sinner. The kingdom of God is in power and not in words or talking.

Stop complaining about those that stood on your way. No one can stand on your way when you know what to do. Remember that you can cause earthquake like Paul and Silas.

.................but the people that do know their God shall be strong, and do exploits.

-Daniel 11:32

You were created to be strong and do exploit. Stop crying! It is written weep not! You are not meant to cry, you are meant to be in command. You

> **You are not meant to cry, you are meant to be in command.**

are meant to be strong and to do exploit. The devil attacks you with depression, murmuring and complains because he wants to drain your strength; he knows that exploits are impossible without strength. Strength only comes on the platform of prayer.

The church

> **The church is the most powerful organisation in the world.**

The church is the most powerful organisation in the world. Everything submits when the church takes its rightful position. Satan cannot shake his body in the face of the church because Christ has already given us the power.

Something happens when the church unite in prayer;

Now about that time Herod the king stretched forth his hands to vex certain of the church. And he killed James the brother of John with the sword. And because he saw it pleased the Jews, he proceeded further to take Peter also. (Then were the days of unleavened bread.) And when he had apprehended him, he put him in prison, and delivered him to four quaternions of soldiers to keep him; intending after Easter to bring him forth to the people. Peter therefore was kept in prison: but prayer was made without ceasing of the church unto God for him. And when Herod would have brought him forth, the same night Peter was sleeping between two soldiers, bound with two chains: and the keepers before the door kept the prison. And, behold, the angel of the Lord came upon him, and a light shined in the prison: and he smote Peter on the side, and raised him up, saying, Arise up quickly. And his chains fell off from his hands. And the angel said unto him, Gird thyself, and bind on thy sandals. And so he did. And he saith unto him, Cast thy garment about thee, and follow me. And he went out, and followed him; and wist not that it was true which was done by the angel; but thought he saw a vision. When they were past the first and the second ward, they came unto the iron gate that leadeth unto the city; which opened to them of his own accord: and they went out, and passed on through one street; and forthwith the angel departed from him. And when Peter was come to himself, he said, Now I know of a surety, that the Lord hath sent his angel, and hath delivered me out of the hand of Herod, and from all the expectation of the people of the Jews.

-Acts 12:1-11

Herod put forth his hand to torment the church of God. He had previously cut-off the head of John the Baptist and had also killed James the brother of John. He continues to peter also, arrested him and put him in prison waiting to be killed.

Herod began to use the church as prey to gain political popularity and admiration from his followers. Thank God there was revival in the church when Peter was arrested and they gathered together to pray. Something happened when the church prayed: God has to send an angel to Peter in prison to bring him out.

But what kind of prayer did the church prayed?

'but prayer was made without ceasing of the church unto God for him'

It was a persistent prayer. They never stop praying until they see Peter's face; though they could not believe probably because of the level of torture the church have previously had from Herod. *Do you know that they are times that the devil will so terrorize one that it will seems as if one's faith is gone?* Yet the church was still able to summon courage and ask for the saving hand of God to bring Peter out and they pray continuously for the release of Peter.

> **When you do what you can do, God will do what you cannot do**

God will do what you cannot do when you do what you can do. They cannot go to the prison to bring out Peter but God can go there. The destiny of Peter would have been shut down if church had shut up.

The church today needs to also constantly pray against the attacks of the devil. The devil will only have upper hand if the church is silent. Satan knows that the church is more powerful if they unite and that is why he constantly attacks the church but we had overcome. Even the least of us had overcome in Jesus name, but we need to continue in prayer to secure the victory we got.

Let the priests, the ministers of the LORD, weep between the porch and the altar, and let them say, Spare thy people, O LORD, and give not thine heritage to reproach, that the heathen should rule over them: wherefore should they say among the people, Where is their God?

- Joel 2:17

We need to constantly pray and weep as priest and ministers of God that the Lord should spare the church; we need to pray out reproach from the church. Today the church seems to be mocked because we are not praying. It is the responsibility of every one of us to pray and weep between the pew and the pulpit, the porch and the alter because we are all priest and ministers of God;

But ye are a chosen generation, a royal priesthood, an holy nation, a peculiar people; that ye should shew forth the praises of him who hath called you out of darkness into his marvellous light:

-1Peter 2:9

You and I became priest with God the moment we are born again which transforms us from darkness into marvellous light. Know that you are made a priest with God already. *Priest of God or for God was only found in the Old Testament. Now we are priest with him and are seated together with him in heavenly places far above principalities and power.* The power of son-ship now qualifies you to raise your voices and show forth the praise of God by silencing the devil. Anytime you silent the devil the praise of God goes forth.

> Anytime you silent the devil the praise of God goes forth.

The praise of God must have gone forth in the entire city because of the deliverance of Peter. I had thought that it must probably have been the talk of media as at that time. The church must have given the media a sleepless night.

Great thing that our mind cannot comprehend happens when the church prays.

Peter had taught to be seeing a vision until he was brought to a secure place and the angel left him.

When the LORD turned again the captivity of Zion, we were like them that dream

-Psalm 126:1

God is going to surprise you as you pray. Gates of iron will begin to open on its own accord as you engage in prayer but if you shut your mouth the devil will shut you down. If you keep silence, the devil

> **...if you shut your mouth the devil will shut you down.**

will kill your children. It is time to cry out. You will only be able to demonstrate power when you pray.

Even Jesus had no alternative than to be oppressed, afflicted and led as a sheep to the slaughter when he closed His mouth.

He was oppressed, and he was afflicted, yet he opened not his mouth: he is brought as a lamb to the slaughter, and as a sheep before her shearers is dumb, so he openeth not his mouth.

-*Isaiah 53:7*

Though the death of Jesus was for our good, I will like you to note that He has to close His mouth to be afflicted. This implies that there is a correction between your victory and the opening of your mouth.

Victory is based more on how you use your strength than the amount of your strength. The church was initially quite and that gave Herod the opportunity to slaughter John and James.

Any time you close your mouth the devil is about to slaughter your life and destiny.

One of the prices for power is prayer.

The apostle

And, behold, I send the promise of my Father upon you: but tarry ye in the city of Jerusalem, until ye be endued with power from on high.

-Luke 24:49

And when the day of Pentecost was fully come, they were all with one accord in one place. And suddenly there came a sound from heaven as of a rushing mighty wind, and it filled all the house where they were sitting. And there appeared unto them cloven tongues like as of fire, and it sat upon each of them. And they were all filled with the Holy Ghost, and began to speak with other tongues, as the Spirit gave them utterance.

-Acts2:1-4

Though Jesus promised the power of the Holy Spirit, the apostles have to pray to receive them. The promises of God are delivered on the platform of prayer; this is

> **The promises of God are delivered on the platform of prayer.**

because promise is not acceptance, you got to tell God that you will like to partake in what has been promised before you can partake in it.

They were all in one accord in one place on the day of Pentecost. They were in agreement on the day of Pentecost. Prayer of agreement is very powerful; the Holy Spirit will always be present whenever we agree together in prayer.

And he spake a parable unto them to this end, that men ought always to pray, and not to faint; Saying, There was in a city a judge, which feared not God, neither regarded man And there was a widow in that city; and she came unto him, saying, Avenge me of mine adversary. And he would not for a while: but afterward he said within himself, Though I fear not God, nor regard man; Yet because this widow troubleth me, I will avenge her, lest by her continual coming she weary me. And the Lord said, Hear what the unjust judge saith. And shall not God avenge his own elect, which cry day and night unto him, though he bear long with them?

-Luke 18:1-7

Persistent prayer works vengeance. Jesus himself has assured us that if an unjust judge can respond to importunity, will not God avenge his own elect which cry day and night unto him, though He bear long with them? What Jesus said here also implies that we should keep calling on God day and night until we receive.

> **They are certain dimensions of power we cannot access until we fast and pray;**

FASTING

Fasting is one of the ways we can gain access to power. Fasting becomes hunger strike when we engage in it without prayer and study of the word of God.

They are certain dimensions of power we cannot access except we fast and pray;

So He said to them, "This kind can come out by nothing but prayer and fasting."

-Mark 9:29.

There are always 'this kind' situation that respond only to fasting and prayer. Fasting is a spiritual force that uproots every satanic stubborn root. Fasting has to been done according to biblical principle.

Wherefore have we fasted, say they, and thou seest not? Wherefore have we afflicted our soul, and thou takest no knowledge? Behold, in the day of your fast ye find pleasure, and exact all your labours. Behold, ye fast for strife and debate, and to smite with the fist of wickedness: ye shall not fast as ye do this day, to make your voice to be heard on high Is it such a fast that I have chosen? a day for a man to afflict his soul? is it to bow down his head as a bulrush, and to spread sackcloth and ashes under him? wilt thou call this a fast, and an acceptable day to the LORD? Is not this the fast that I have chosen? to loose the bands of wickedness, to undo the heavy burdens, and to let the oppressed go free, and that ye break every yoke? Is it not to deal thy bread to the hungry, and that thou bring the poor that are cast out to thy house? when thou seest the naked, that thou cover him; and that thou hide not thyself from thine own flesh? Then shall thy light break forth as the morning, and thine health shall spring forth speedily: and thy righteousness shall go before thee; the glory of the LORD shall be thy rereward.

-Isaiah 58:3-8

Hypocritical fast never yield any result, it only amount to one afflicting ones soul. Fasting becomes punishment when you engage in cheating, killing and all sort of wickedness while fasting. The fasting that God have ordained is to break the bands of wickedness, remove heavy burden and release the oppressed out of oppression.

This had clearly showed us that fasting is necessary to gain command over wickedness, we are now living in the world of wickedness

.... and the whole world lieth in wickedness.

-1John 5:19

There is so much wickedness in the world today that it will be risky to stay without power. Wicked people are turning beautiful ladies to men; their faces are masked with the face of men so that they cannot marry. Certain people's destinies are buried and they wonder from places to places without direction. Oppression is so common on our street today. Insane people that you see on the street were not created by God that way; some wicked powers caused it, the high number of the unemployed flooding the street today is due to the oppression of the devil, religious attacks on the church that we see today is satanic wickedness, emerging sickness and diseases are heavy burdens from the pit of hell, not to even talk about our society that is becoming anti-Christ on a daily basis. We need to be empowered on the platform of prayer and fasting to be able to gain command against all the wickedness of the devil.

Without fasting we cannot gain command to declare the acceptable day of the LORD, we will not be able to preach the kingdom of God effectively and we will not be able to command deliverance in the life of people. Fasting is what empowers one to be able to give a dead line to afflictions and all the works of the devil. Your words will sound like an empty barrel to the devil without power.

Any true story of any great men and women were born out of fierce fasting and prayer engagement.

When you fast try to be kind to people, make everyone around you happy, then you will discover that your health will spring forth speedily, righteousness will become your lifestyle and you will begin to operate in God's glory. Fasting cannot kill anybody neither will it make you seek, there is healing power in fasting, do not allow the devil to deceive you;

> **Fasting cannot kill anybody neither will it make you seek, there is healing power in fasting, do not allow the devil to deceive you;**

When I was about to take a substantial step toward my ministry, I saw that God will want me to fast for certain period of time. As I was about to start, I had a very serious sudden asthmatic attack which I have never experienced neither was it found in my family history. I was also afflicted with sudden heart failure and weakness. This infirmity was so terrible that words cannot describe how I felt. I latter relocated to the United Kingdom for my doctorate degree and that gave me the opportunity to seek better medical attention. Several tests were done on me and nothing seems to be wrong with me yet I was not myself.

I started the fasting and after a week the asthmatic attack became so fierce and strong, unfortunately I have to stop the fasting. The burden to start the fasting again came so strongly some weeks after, this time I started the fasting by faith. Two weeks into the fasting the attack came again; I refused to end the fasting this time. I said if I perish I perish. Now I know that those that say so never perish. It was so terrible but I refused to give up. It happened that when the devil sees that I am determined and no longer afraid of death he left me alone.

Fasting actually heal the body. Sometimes the devil brings infirmity to keep you from operating in the fullness of your divine destiny but when you ignore his tricks and lay hold on spiritual biblical principles you will definitely gain victory over him.

But they that wait upon the LORD shall renew their strength; they shall mount up with wings as eagles; they shall run, and not be weary; and they shall walk, and not faint.

-Isaiah 40:31

You can see from the light of the scripture that waiting upon the Lord renews ones strength. It makes you to mount up wings like an eagle. Unusual strength is delivered on the platform of fasting. I am usually strengthened each time I fast. Sometimes, I will be tired after fasting throughout the day but I will become strengthened the moment I began to pray.

Now I will look at my present life and screened: *no one has this kind of strength on earth except me!* The dying asthmatic boy is now like a valiant army. Praise the Lord!

Jesus: our perfect example

And when he had fasted forty days and forty nights, he was afterward an hungred.

-Mathew 4:2

Jesus being the Son of God fasted. This was someone representing the interest of heaven, yet He fasted. If Jesus can fast to succeed in ministry, how dare you think that you need not fast to fulfil destiny.

> **It is natural for one to become hungry during fasting but that does not mean weakness**

It is natural for one to become hungry during fasting but that does not mean weakness. *Weakness is different from being hungry, so, never think that you are weak when you are hungry. A weak person can be easily defeated but a hungry person can be more violent. Satan came to Jesus thinking that hunger means weakness and he thought that he could defeat Jesus but he lost out.*

And when the tempter came to him, he said, If thou be the Son of God, command that these stones be made bread. But he answered and said, It is written, Man shall not live by bread alone, but by every word that proceedeth out of the mouth of God.

-Mathew 4:3-4

When you fast you are empowered to overcome the temptation of the devil. Fasting silence the flesh and empower your Spirit making you to gain victory over the assault and embarrassments of satan.

Jesus ministry was so successful because He fasted and that explain why they could not touch Him before His time. No one can cut your destiny short if you are truly engaged in fasting. You will rather cut down the devil than cutting you down.

Moses

The ministry of Moses was so successful because he fasted. His face was shining after he came down from the mount. Moses did not know that his face was shining but other people saw it.

> **There are transformations that take place in your life each time you truly engage in fasting.**

Whether you know it or not there are transformations that take place in your life each time you truly engage in fasting.

And he was there with the LORD forty days and forty nights; he did neither eat bread, nor drink water. And he wrote upon the tables the words of the covenant, the Ten Commandments. And it came to pass, when Moses came down from mount Sinai with the two tables of testimony in Moses' hand, when he came down from the mount, that Moses wist not that the skin of his face shone while he talked with him.

-Exodus 34:28-29

It was on the platform of fasting that God gave Moses the commandment. He was engrafted in the word of God during the forty days and forty nights and was busy writing the commandments.

Moses face was shining because God do speak with him face to face.

And the LORD spake unto Moses face to face, as a man speaketh unto his friend......

- Exodus 33:11.

When you rub minds with God and commune with Him your face will definitely shine.

Moses was so relaxed in the presence of the Lord for forty days and forty nights, a lot of people will want to turn the hand of the clock on the day of their fast. They will not be patient to pray, they are only eager to eat food and break their fast. That you stayed from 6a.m to12 noon or 6p.m without food does not make that a fast. It will only amount to hunger strike if you do not settle down to seek the face of God.

When you seek the face of God and rub mind with Him, the devil will be afraid to look at your face let alone attack you. I have noticed that when the demon possessed sees me they bow their head and look down, some of them run literarily. A lady once saw me and it was like my presence was fire to her, I watched her as she was struggling to run away from me with all effort, not wanting to look at my face after preaching to her.

Henceforth, satan will run away from you in Jesus name. As you are reading this book you are being empowered and your face will begin to shine in the mighty name of Jesus.

FAITH

Faith is a very strong weapon that delivers power. Faith is a warfare weapon designed in God's armoury. Faith is an abstract noun according to men's English but it is actually seen and felt.

For whatsoever is born of God overcometh the world: and this is the victory that overcometh the world, even our faith.

-1John 5:4

Faith is equal to victory. Faith is the victory that overcomes the world meaning that your faith is actually the victory that you have over the devil. *When your faith is in place your victory will be in place. If your faith says yes God will not say no!* If it has not worked for you then it was not faith you had. Faith cannot fail. God designed faith in His factory in heaven and released it to you. Faith is the quencher of all the affliction of the devil, it helps you to gain command in the realm of the Spirit and in the physical. Faith is the shield you have over all the assault of the devil. It is your defence and when your faith is not in place you become vulnerable to the devil.

Above all, taking the shield of faith, wherewith ye shall be able to quench all the fiery darts of the wicked.

-Ephesians 6:16

Faith is above all. It is above all those alternatives you have tried and failed, it quenches all the fire of the enemy not even one of the devil strategy and oppression could escape the power of faith. *Without faith you remain powerless no matter who you are*. Faith is what guarantees your security and sustenance in a hostile environment.

The above passage said with faith you will be able to quench all the fiery darts of the wicked. This implies that faith enables. It enables you to conquer.

But without faith it is impossible to please him: for he that cometh to God must believe that he is, and that he is a rewarder of them that diligently seek him.

Hebrews 11:6

Without faith it is impossible, everything is impossible without faith. If you cannot please God without faith, it then means that you cannot get anything from God without faith.

But Jesus beheld them, and said unto them, With men this is impossible; but with God all things are possible.

- Mathew 19:26

For verily I say unto you, That whosoever shall say unto this mountain, Be thou removed, and be thou cast into the sea; and shall not doubt in his heart, but shall believe that those things which he saith shall come to pass; he shall have whatsoever he saith.

Mark 11:23

Looking at Mathew 19:26 above you will noticed that certain things are only possible to God but when you read Mark 11:23 you will notice that whosoever (including yourself) can have whatsoever (anything) he/she says when he/she believed (faith). This implies that *faith puts you in the same class as God.*

All things are not only possible to God but also to whosoever believes in God.

Men can look at your status but faith does not look at your status. Faith is whosoever, it does not consider your personality, class of degree, family history, the bible school you attend, your business or church location, how much money you have and whether you have people encouraging you or not. Faith does not consider all that. Faith is only interested in lifting whosoever to whatever class or status they desire.

'Whosoever shall say'; God's word in His mouth is as potent as His word in your mouth through faith. The faith that works is the faith that both speaks and works.

-------- but the just shall live by his faith

- Habakkuk 2:4

The just can only live by faith, not even the faith of his/her pastor but **his** faith. Those that got healed in the ministry of Jesus were healed because of their faith. The evidence is all over the scripture, here is just one;

And Jesus said unto him, Go thy way; ***thy faith*** *hath made thee whole. And immediately he received his sight, and followed Jesus in the way.*

- Mark 10:52 (Bolden, mine)

270

The just can only be empowered by **his** faith.

You did not suffer lose when you lose your blessing, you lose when you lost your faith because your faith will always get back your blessing. If you lost your faith you have no reason to exist. That is why you must fight to retain your faith.

Fight the good fight of faith..........................

- 1 Timothy 6:12.

The fight for your faith is a very good fight. You fight to keep your faith by making out time to attend bible teaching and all avenues that make you hear from God because faith comes by hearing from God. You fight the good fight of faith by fighting discouragement.

Your life, business, ministry and whatever God has called you to do can be transformed through faith.

By faith Enoch was translated that he should not see death; and was not found, because God had translated him: for before his translation he had this testimony, that he pleased God.-Hebrews 11:5

Faith can translate from sickness to health, poverty to wealth, struggling to empowerment and lots more. Faith cannot see corruption (death). You cannot die in that sickness if you can believe God. You cannot suffer loose in that business if you can believe God. Faith translates you from seeing death.

For by it (faith) the elders obtained a good report.

- Hebrews 11:2. Bracket, mine.

To follow example is a fast way of solving mathematical problems. The challenges of life are mathematical in nature. They all have solution but those that lack the right example and formula will always struggle and suffer, they will always believe that life is difficult. That is why people commit suicide. Friends! Life to me is exciting and worth living.

You can enjoy life much more than I do if you can follow the examples of the elders that have obtained good report through faith. The scripture above tells us how these elders obtained good report. They obtained it through faith.

272

Faith can obtain anything you want. There cannot be any testimony of empowerment without faith.

Faith mechanism of action

Faith is difficult for people to have because they do not know how faith works. A lot of people always think; how will God do it? They try to imagine how it will come to pass, through that the devil attacks their faith. They have a wrong understanding about the force of faith. Many people thought that God is going to move or create something afresh when they exhibit faith. The devil will lose out if you can understand that all what you needed and will ever need is already created and made available. Your faith is not going to move God anew because God is already moved. He is done with whatever you need and whatever you will ever need. He has finished all the work, for He said, *it is finished*. Faith gives you access to everything that God has already provided. Your faith is not going to make God create anything again for they were already

> **Your faith is not going to move God anew because God is already moved.**

created for you. Faith only gives you access to what God has created for you.

According as his divine power hath given unto us all things that pertain unto life and godliness, through the knowledge of him that hath called us to glory and virtue:

-2Peter 1:3

He has already given us all things that pertained to life (material things) and godliness (righteousness) and we gain access to these things through His knowledge. Knowledge comes through the study of the word of God, which brings faith in us. Knowledge is not a gift. You must study to gain knowledge.

Blessed be the God and Father of our Lord Jesus Christ, who hath blessed us with all spiritual blessings in heavenly places in Christ: According as he hath chosen us in him before the foundation of the world, that we should be holy and without blame before him in love: -Ephesians 1:3-4.

> **Unbelief causes death and a lot of people have died of unbelief more than cancer and HIV/AIDS put together.**

God has already blessed us with all spiritual blessing. If you are blessed in the realm of the spirit it must manifest in the physical because the spiritual creates the physical. We were already blessed!

For we are his workmanship, created in Christ Jesus unto good works, which God hath before ordained that we should walk in them

-Ephesians 2:10

God has already created us unto good works in Christ Jesus and we are meant to walk in them.

So much power has been made available to us and we can lay hand on them only through faith.

Faith is the only condition to the realm of possibility. It is written '*Only believe*'. If you believe you cannot perish. Unbelief causes death; a lot of people have died of unbelief more than both cancer and HIV/AIDS.

For God so loved the world, that he gave his only begotten Son, that whosoever believeth in him should not perish, but have everlasting life.

-John 3:16

Believing guarantees your access to freedom from death, cancer, HIV/AIDs, delay in marriage, unemployment and many more. *If you believe you cannot perish.*

It is wisdom to believe and avoid being swallowed by the powers of wickedness.

Faith please God and when God is pleased with you there is no limit to the amount of His blessing that you will both enjoy and command.

It is time to demonstrate the effective force of faith. You know the value of a thing from its usage. If you got this faith in you then put it to work.

Time can never be enough to describe the potential and effective force of faith. With faith you can stop the mouth of lions, wrought righteousness, and subdue kingdoms.

And what shall I more say? for the time would fail me to tell of Gedeon, and of Barak, and of Samson, and of Jephthae; of David also, and Samuel, and of the prophets:

Who through faith subdued kingdoms, wrought righteousness, obtained promises, stopped the mouths of lions, Quenched the violence of fire, escaped the edge of the sword, out of weakness were made strong, waxed valiant in fight, turned to flight the armies of the aliens. Women received their dead raised to life again: and others were tortured, not accepting deliverance; that they might obtain a better resurrection:

-Hebrew 11:32-35

It is time to release the fire of faith.

SACRIFICE

I have studied so many businessmen, women, student, farmers and ministers of God and I realised that the level of sacrifice they made determines the level of their success. There cannot be any true story of empowerment without sacrifice.

Sacrifice is different from normal offering that you know, though sacrifice is also a form of offering. In a simple term sacrifice is painful giving. It is giving a very costly and something dare to you to God.

The children of Israel understand what sacrifice is all about;

And Pharaoh called for Moses and Aaron, and said, Go, sacrifice to your God [here] in the land [of Egypt].

And Moses said, It is not suitable or right to do that; for the animals the Egyptians hold sacred and will not permit to be slain are those which we are accustomed to sacrifice to the Lord our God; if we did this before the eyes of the Egyptians, would they not stone us? We will go a three days' journey into the wilderness and sacrifice to the Lord our God, as He will command us.

Exodus 8:25-27

The animals that the Egyptian hold sacred and are abomination to be slain by the Egyptian are the ones the children of Israel are accustomed to sacrifice to the Lord.

They are accustomed to giving them. It had become their lifestyle. It was a customary thing to them.

Sacrifice is giving what other people cannot give. When people by chance get to know the kind of sacrifice I make, they were like, are you crazy? The world and ignorant believers call sacrifice foolishness.

It is not said to be sacrifice until you give that which seems to be a crazy thing to men. Moses said to Pharoah, would the Egyptian not stone us if we try sacrificing before them? Have people ever tried to stone you for sacrificing unto God, either with your body, time, money or material things? People that do not understand will always want to stone you.

The statement of Moses also implies that the Egyptians are not aware of the kind of sacrifice the children of Israel were accustomed to giving unto God. Know that *having what to eat and drink is not prosperity but survival.* To experience prosperity you need the secret. It is not a secret just for the sake of being a secret but a secret because many people will not like to hear it. They will rather stone you if you dear tell them to do it. So, people are scared of saying it out therefore it remains a secret to them.

Don't you know that there are some anointed men of God that hardly talk about giving let alone sacrifice? Not because they don't want to but because the people will easily take them to be fake.

People that are blessed did uncommon things to be blessed. Can you see the secret of the continuous favour and blessings among the children of Israel? Can you see their secret of victory over their enemy?

Until you give God what you have He cannot give you what you don't have.

Understand also that sacrifice must be made according to the commandment of the Lord. Moses said '*as He will command us.*' So, sacrifice must be done in accordance to the commandment of the Lord. You don't sacrifice to please the pastor you sacrifice to please God.

God taught me the power of sacrifice while I was in year two in the university. It happened that I was left with little amount money (just 20NGN) at the middle of the semester. This money cannot buy anything to satisfy me. I went down to buy bean cake but could not because the money can only buy 4 small pieces of bean cake, which I definitely know it will not satisfy me and I wouldn't like to lose the money because at least I am holding something. I later decided to take the money to the church. The following day my phone rang and when I picked it up it was good news of 20,000NGN transferred into my account by someone who has never given me money. After that day sacrifice became my lifestyle.

Know that it is not only money that you can sacrifice. You can sacrifice your time; say in the service of God or in prayer and fasting. Whenever you create time amidst your busy schedule, it is a kind of sacrifice.

Sacrifice actually gives you access to divine open cheque.

And Solomon went up thither to the brasen altar before the LORD, which was at the tabernacle of the congregation, and offered a thousand burnt offerings upon it. In that night did God appear unto Solomon, and said unto him, Ask what I shall give thee.

-2 Chronicle1:6-7.

When Solomon offered a thousand offering to God, He appeared unto him in the dream giving him an open check. The greatness and life history of Solomon is not unconnected with his sacrifice.

Sacrifice is releasing a thousand worth of an offering (thousands of offering). It is the highest form of giving. That is why God sacrificed Jesus, His only begotten son.

Sacrifice is giving all or something very dear or useful to you to God. It is giving your best, prompt giving and giving whole-heartedly.

The sacrifice of Abraham

Abraham was tested by God to offer up Isaac and He made no hesitation at all. He knows that God that gave him Isaac will be able to raise him up again even if he slaughtered him to God. The faith of Abraham in God is what motivated his action. Without faith and love we cannot offer unto God.

And it came to pass after these things, that God did tempt Abraham, and said unto him, Abraham: and he said, Behold, here I am. And he said, Take now thy son, thine only son Isaac, whom thou lovest, and get thee into the land of Moriah; and offer him there for a burnt offering upon one of the mountains which I will tell thee of. And Abraham rose up early in the morning, and saddled his ass, and took two of his young men with him, and Isaac his son, and clave the wood for the

283

burnt offering, and rose up, and went unto the place of which God had told him. Then on the third day Abraham lifted up his eyes, and saw the place afar off. And Abraham said unto his young men, Abide ye here with the ass; and I and the lad will go yonder and worship, and come again to you. And Abraham took the wood of the burnt offering, and laid it upon Isaac his son; and he took the fire in his hand, and a knife; and they went both of them together. And Isaac spake unto Abraham his father, and said, My father: and he said, Here am I, my son. And he said, Behold the fire and the wood: but where is the lamb for a burnt offering? And Abraham said, My son, God will provide himself a lamb for a burnt offering: so they went both of them together. And they came to the place which God had told him of; and Abraham built an altar there, and laid the wood in order, and bound Isaac his son, and laid him on the altar upon the wood. And Abraham stretched forth his hand, and took the knife to slay his son. And the angel of the LORD called unto him out of heaven, and said, Abraham, Abraham: and he said, Here am I. And he said, Lay not thine hand upon the lad, neither do thou anything unto him: for now I know that thou fearest God, seeing thou hast not withheld thy son, thine only son from me. And Abraham lifted up his eyes, and looked, and behold behind him a ram caught in a thicket by his horns: and Abraham went and took the ram, and offered him up for a burnt offering in the stead of his son. And Abraham called the name of that place Jehovah jireh: as it is said to this day, In the mount of the LORD it shall be seen.

-Genesis 22:1-14

You can again understand what sacrifice is from the above scripture. God tested Abraham to take his only son whom he love and offer him in the place

> **It is one thing to give sacrificially and also another thing to give rightly.**

that he will show him in the region of Moriah. Sacrifice therefore is giving to God that which might be the only thing that you have and that is so dear to you.

Note that in giving your sacrifice you give according to the instruction that God will give you as said earlier.

It was God that chooses for Abraham the region to offer the offering. He told him to go to mount Moriah. It is one thing to give sacrificially and also another thing to give rightly. Sacrifice can be rejected when it is not offered in the right place. A lot of people give sacrificially but they sow in a non-fertile ground. God knows where the ground is fertile for you to offer your sacrifice. If it is not offered in the place that the Lord shall choose it will not germinate.

But unto the place which the LORD your God shall choose out of all your tribes to put his name there, even unto his habitation shall ye seek, and thither thou shalt come: And thither ye shall bring your burnt offerings, and your sacrifices, and your tithes, and heave offerings of your hand, and your vows, and your freewill offerings, and the firstlings of your herds and of your flocks:

-Deuteronomy 12:5-6

Instruction is what makes a high flyer. One beautiful thing about the sacrifice of Abraham is that he offered according to the instruction, as I will be sharing with you shortly. There are places you offer your sacrifice and it will command generational power and protection.

Abraham did not hesitate as the bible recorded that he rose early in the morning, saddled his donkey, and took his young men and his son Isaac. *Whenever God tell you to do a thing, act promptly because your blessing is in it.* When you hesitate the devil will come and confuse you. The Bible did not record that Abraham made any consultation with his wife. It is good to commune with your husband or wife but your blessing could be hindered if your spouse goes against the instruction of the Lord. As for me I thank God for my wife because when I say darling God want this or that, her response is always glory be to God. Every instruction from God is to be followed promptly.

I understood that the region of Moriah where God choose for Abraham to offer up Isaac was far from where he lived. The bible recorded that Abraham took

287

off immediately he rose up in the morning. In verse 4 of Genesis 22, the bible said on the third day he looked up and saw the place at a distance meaning that it took Abraham about three days journey to get close to the place of sacrifice. What must have Abraham and Isaac been thinking for all these three days?

I am surprised that Abraham did not change his mind. The devil must have come to him within this period to say Abraham, are you crazy? Why will you want to kill the child, your only son in the name of sacrificial offer unto God, don't you know how long you waited to get him?

Sometimes you hear from God and as time passes you allow the devil to water it down and the excitement and enthusiasm you had as at the time of the revelation automatically died down because satan knows that your prosperity is in the voice and instruction that you have received from the Lord.

Abraham must have been very focused on the faithfulness of God; he must have thought that though he sacrifices the child, God is able to raise him up again. Abraham knows that the God he had encountered and walked with all these days cannot fail. Abraham could trust God because He had walked with Him all this years.

> **It is not just enough to believe that God can do all things but your life is going to change when you know that God can do all things for you.**

If you do not have a relationship with God you will find it difficult to offer unto God and if you do not offer sacrificially unto God, there are certain realms of power that you cannot access.

. Abel offered a more excellent sacrifice than Cain because Abel had a relationship and faith in God. Faith in God means confidence that God can do all things. When you have that mentality that God can do all things and that he can do all things for you then you will not find it difficult to offer sacrificially unto God. There are

> **Love for God is the foundation of being able to offer sacrificially unto God**

people that believe that God can do all things but they never have that confidence that God can do all things for them. It is not just enough to believe that God can do all things but your life is going to change when you know that God can do all things for you.

By faith Abel offered unto God a more excellent sacrifice than Cain, by which he obtained witness that he was righteous, God testifying of his gifts: and by it he being dead yet speaketh.

-Hebrew 11:4

> **If you touch God heart God will touch your heart too.**

The confidence that you have in God is what creates the platform for you to offer sacrificially unto God. There are good sacrifices, there are

> **The most secured form of saving and insurance is to give sacrificially.**

better sacrifices, there are excellent sacrifices and there are more excellent sacrifices. Abel operated in the highest level of sacrifice because he had faith in God.

Abel gave something that touched God to the extent that God testified of his gift. If you touch God's heart God will touch your heart too.

There are dimensions of sacrifice that can speak even after death. Sacrifices never die. The most secured form of saving and insurance is to give sacrificially.

The sacrifice of Abel was speaking even after he slept. Your sacrifice can continue to speak even after you sleep. Abel's blood was speaking after he slept. The Bible said there is life in the blood meaning that Abel is not dead but sleeping because dead people cannot have life in their blood. For a blood to speak implies the presence of life. In other word the sacrifice of Abel gave life to him even after he slept.

They are people that are 'dead' physically but are still living because of their works and there are people that are living but are as good as dead (*But she that liveth in pleasure is dead while she liveth-1Timothy 5:6*). '*Only one life that will soon be gone only work done for Christ that will last*'.

Significance of Abraham's Sacrifice

The sacrifice of Abraham has generation-to-generation effect. Remember that Abraham eventually did not sacrifice Isaac. God told him not to harm the child and when he looked up, he offered a ram instead.

Note that the ram Abraham offered has a very big significant effect upon Israel and the Church.

What is a ram? A ram is an uncastrated male sheep. Note also that when an animal is castrated, the seed are destroyed and cannot reproduce.

Also note that Jesus was led as a lamb to the slaughter and sheep before her shearers;

He was oppressed, and he was afflicted, yet he opened not his mouth: he is brought as a lamb to the slaughter, and as a sheep before her shearers is dumb, so he openeth not his mouth.

-Isaiah 53:7

Understand also that a lamb is a baby sheep.

Now, the ram that Abraham offered symbolizes the death of Jesus. Jesus was the uncastrated Lamb of God that died for us on the cross of Calvary to take away our sins.

The next day John seeth Jesus coming unto him, and saith, Behold the Lamb of God, which taketh away the sin of the world

-John 1:29

Note that when Isaac asked Abraham; 'where is the lamb for the sacrifice' He replied that God would provide for himself a lamb for the sacrifice (Genesis 22:8), that was a prophetic utterance unknown to Abraham. I do not think that Abraham fully understood the implication of this prophecy and the act of sacrificing the Ram.

That Ram was indeed the symbol of Jesus coming to die for us on the mountain of Calvary. Jesus died with all of our sin upon him because all have sin and have come short of the glory of God (Roman 3:23). We all were in Jesus as a symbol of sin and He went to the cross to crucify our sins there, which is in line with the un-castrated lamb that Abraham, sacrificed.

The sacrifice of Abraham was indeed the symbol of Jesus death which happened long ago in the realm of the spirit before the physical manifestation of it on the cross; Let me prove what I have said to you: the bible says by His stripes we were healed;

Who his own self bare our sins in his own body on the tree, that we, being dead to sins, should live unto righteousness: by whose stripes ye were healed.

-1Peter 2:24

But he was wounded for our transgressions; he was bruised for our iniquities: the chastisement of our peace was upon him; and with his stripes we are healed.

-Isaiah 53:5

When was his stripes that healed the woman with the issue of blood and when was his stripes that healed the blind man?

Jesus was able to do all these miracles because he was slain and striped (flogged) from the foundation of the world and the death on the cross was just a physical manifestation.

And all that dwell upon the earth shall worship him, whose names are not written in the book of life of the **Lamb slain from the foundation of the world.**

-Revelation 13:8 (bold mine)

Jesus was slain from the foundation of the earth because he loved us from the foundation of the earth. He gave

295

His begotten son from the foundation of the earth and He Choose us from the foundation of the world.

According as he hath chosen us in him before the foundation of the world, that we should be holy and without blame before him in love:

-Ephesians 1:4 (bolden, mine)

*For we which have believed do enter into rest, as he said, as I have sworn in my wrath, if they shall enter into my rest: **although the works were finished from the foundation of the world.***

-Hebrew 4:3 (bolden, mine)

*When Jesus therefore had received the vinegar, he said, **It is finished**: and he bowed his head, and gave up the ghost.*

John 19:30 (bolden, mine)

The works were finished from the foundation of the world in a spiritual realm before Jesus came to demonstrate it physically.

Jesus has to come physically to show what has been accomplished spiritually because not everyone understands the realm of the Spirit. He came to physically show what has been accomplished spiritually so that He can give men understanding of what has been done in the spiritual realm so that we can have access to the salvation.

Note that Salvation itself is a Spiritual thing; and those that are truly born again knows the transformation that has taken place in their spirit. The physical manifestation of the redemptive work of grace therefore is to make us gain access to the realm of the Spirit, the salvation of our soul.

That which is born of the flesh is flesh; and that which is born of the Spirit is spirit.

-John 3:6.

I took time to explain all these things so that you can have the understanding of how far sacrifice can go.

Nothing delivers the mercy and favour of God like sacrifice. Sacrifice gives you automatic access to God; it makes you obtain divine witness or testimony like Abel (Hebrew 11:4). What happened during the baptism of Jesus (Matthew 17:5.) showed us the importance of this divine witness or testimony. Everyone that has that divine witness of God in him is to be heard. Sacrifice is one of the platform on which divine approval can be delivered.

Sacrifice can protect from death; when satan motivated David to number Israel, God was displeased and He told David through his seer, Gad that he (David) should choose from some list of punishments;

So Gad came to David, and said unto him, Thus saith the LORD, Choose thee Either three years' famine; or three months to be destroyed before thy foes, while that the sword of thine enemies overtaketh thee; or else three days the sword of the LORD, even the pestilence, in the land, and the angel of the LORD destroying throughout all the coasts of Israel. Now therefore advise thyself what word I shall bring again to him that sent me. And David said unto Gad, I am in a great strait: let me fall now into the hand of the LORD; for very great are his mercies: but let me not fall into the hand of man. So the LORD sent pestilence upon Israel: and there fell of Israel seventy thousand men. And God sent an angel unto Jerusalem to destroy it: and as he was destroying, the LORD beheld, and he repented him of the evil, and said to the angel that destroyed, It is enough, stay now thine hand. And the angel of the LORD stood by the threshingfloor of Ornan the Jebusite.

-1 Chronicles 21:11-15

David decided that it will be better to fall into the hand of God than man, and the Lord send an angel into Jerusalem to destroy and when the Angel came to the threshing floor of Ornan the Jebusite he stood and stop destroying.

Where is this threshing flour of Ornan the Jebusite and why did the angel of the Lord stops destroying?

Mount Moriah was the designated threshing floor of Araunah the Jebusite according to the scripture;

Then Solomon began to build the house of the LORD at Jerusalem in mount Moriah, where the LORD appeared unto David his father, in the place that David had prepared in the threshingfloor of Ornan the Jebusite.

-2 Chronicles 3:1

Note that Ornan was also called Araunah, the scripture below will convince you as David was commanded to build a house for God at the threshing floor of Ornan the Jebusite which was also referred to as the threshing floor of Araunah the Jebusite by the same prophet (seer), Gad.

And Gad came that day to David, and said unto him, Go up, rear an altar unto the LORD in the threshingfloor of Araunah the Jebusite.

-2Samuel 24:18

Then the angel of the LORD commanded Gad to say to David, that David should go up, and set up an altar

300

unto the LORD in the threshingfloor of Ornan the Jebusite.

-2 Chronicles 21:18

You can see from the above scriptures that mount Moriah was the threshing floor of Ornan the Jebusite.

The angel of the Lord stopped destroying because God remembered the sacrifice of His friend Abraham and He was pleased.

Our God is a God that cannot forget our labour of love because God is not wicked and God is not unrighteous.

For God is not unrighteous to forget your work and labour of love, which ye have showed toward his name, in that ye have ministered to the saints, and do minister.

-Hebrew 6:10

God still remembered the sacrifice of Abraham even after many years. There are certain things that you will do that will make God to bless you from generation to generation.

Most of the problem people are facing today is as a result of generational curse. *Know that Just as you are aware that curse can move from generation to generation; know also that blessing can move from generation to generation.* The blessing that follows sacrifice can erase the curse of death or punishment placed upon you and your family line.

The king of Moab

Do you know that our God is a Jealous God? Seven places of the bible recorded that our God is a Jealous God;

For thou shalt worship no other god: for the LORD, whose name is Jealous, is a jealous God:

-Exodus 34:14

For the LORD thy God is a consuming fire, even a jealous God.

-Deuteronomy 4:24

I was in a taxi in the northern part of Nigeria going for my prayer meeting and they was this Muslim religious fanatic in his religious attire that sat sanctimoniously beside me. The Holy Spirit told me to look at this man and as I looked He asked me a question that; assuming there is a challenge or battle between you and this man right now, do you think you will be able to conquer him? As I was about to reply Him He said to me that, if the consecration of this man to his god is more than your consecration to your God, you will not be able to conquer him and I was very shocked!

Do you know that they are many believers today that are being tormented by the witches and wizard and they are even running for them? Some believers are even afraid to visit their hometown. Some are more afraid and naive in the society than unbelievers when we should be as bold as lion.

303

Many so called believers today are being afflicted by the wicked ones in occultism and witchcraft meetings, why? It is because the consecrations/devotion of those people to their gods (their witchcraft meeting and their cultism) is more powerful than your consecration and devotion to God almighty.

So many believers do not know how to offer sacrifice and thanksgiving to God. People in the witchcraft societies are told to donate their children and they obey, occult people that drinks human blood pay serious devotion to their god but believers are careless and God is Jealous about this thing.

I will like to show you a story in the Bible about the war between Israel and the Moabites;

But it came to pass, when Ahab was dead, that the king of Moab rebelled against the king of Israel..........And he went and sent to Jehoshaphat the king of Judah, saying, The king of Moab hath rebelled against me: wilt thou go with me against Moab to battle? And he said, I will go up: I am as thou art, my people as thy

people, and my horses as thy horses...........But Jehoshaphat said, Is there not here a prophet of the LORD, that we may enquire of the LORD by him? And one of the king of Israel's servants answered and said, Here is Elisha the son of Shaphat, which poured water on the hands of Elijah. And Jehoshaphat said, The word of the LORD is with him. So the king of Israel and Jehoshaphat and the king of Edom went down to him........... 14 And Elisha said, As the LORD of hosts liveth, before whom I stand, surely, were it not that I regard the presence of Jehoshaphat the king of Judah, I would not look toward thee, nor see thee. But now bring me a minstrel. And it came to pass, when the minstrel played, that the hand of the LORD came upon him. And he said, Thus saith the LORD, Make this valley full of ditches. For thus saith the LORD, Ye shall not see wind, neither shall ye see rain; yet that valley shall be filled with water, that ye may drink, both ye, and your cattle, and your beasts. And this is but a light thing in the sight of the LORD: he will deliver the Moabites also into your hand. And ye shall smite every fenced city, and every choice city, and shall fell every good tree, and stop all wells of water, and mar every good piece of land with stones ....And they rose up early in the morning, and the sun shone upon the water, and the Moabites saw the water on the other side as red as blood: And they said, This is blood: the kings are surely slain, and they have smitten one another: now therefore, Moab, to the spoil. And when they came to the camp of Israel, the Israelites rose up and smote the Moabites, so that they fled before them: but they went forward smiting the Moabites, even in their country.....And when the king of Moab saw that the battle was too sore for him, he took with him seven hundred men that drew swords, to break through even unto the king of Edom: but they could not. Then he took his eldest son that should have reigned in his stead, and offered him for a burnt offering upon the wall. And there was great indignation against Israel: and they departed from him, and returned to their own land.

-2 King 3:5, 7, 11, 12, 14-19, 22-24, 26-27

306

> **Have you ever thought of giving sacrificially to God amidst your prosperity and the goodness of God that you have been enjoying?**

Note the point I want to make here; God promised Israel through the prophet that they were going to win. Yes! They were actually winning according to the word of God but they never win to the end because they failed to give thanks to God. They were careless. *The heathen king understood the power of sacrifice but the children of Israel neither understand sacrifice nor thanksgiving, they took God for granted.*

When God saw what the king of Moab did for his god by sacrificing his only son who is to become an heir He became jealous and forsook the children of Israel and there was a great indignation against Israel that they turned their back before their enemy.

Have you ever thought of giving sacrificially to God amidst your prosperity and the goodness of God that you have been enjoying? It was prophesied to you that you would succeed but do you care to give God something

> **..You cannot overcome your enemy all this while because they are more devoted to their god than your devotion to your God**

since you were succeeding? You need to be wise and learn from the word of God.

For whatsoever things were written aforetime were written for our learning, that we through patience and comfort of the scriptures might have hope.

-Roman 15:4.

God is a jealous God. You cannot overcome your enemy all this while because they are more devoted to their god than your devotion to your God. You have the opportunity today to start winning based on this revelation that I have shared with you.

It is wisdom to sow a sacrificial seed for any prophecy you receive and every step of victory you got. It is only then that your continuous victory will be guaranteed. Many people that had started well today ended badly because they did not understand the biblical principle of sacrifice. It is not uncommon to see people that are succeeding and booming initially only to begin to experience a fall suddenly without any reason known to them. It is because they forgot God and abandoned him. Their enemies who are more devoted to their god then launched an attack against them and that is why they are finding it difficult to survive, that is why some businesses are dead and that is why many are under the bondage of sicknesses and diseases until now.

There was a day I took all the money that I have home and bank and take everything to the Church of God, my wife was about 4 months pregnant for my first child as at that time. We went to church with the money that day not having what we will be coming back to eat at home. That day my wife was craving to eat yam. It happened that as we dropped the money at the altar that day someone gave us some tubers of yam from the church. By July my salary was increased by over 3 times and backdated to about a year. Praise the Lord!

These blessings I have received taught me how to do more sacrifice. I again bundled some significant amount of money to the church and shortly after that day, God opened the door of international opportunity for me and I became an international champion; I was invited to Germany for an interview and it was about what I never studied, I saw myself competing with people that are more experienced than me; they came from all over the world, Africa, America, Europe, South America and Asia. I seem to be the only one that attended primitive school in an underdeveloped country among them. But the anointing of God that has been working excellence in me and the power of sacrifice that have become my lifestyle distinguished me. I was chosen above them and given the fellowship.

After I got this fellowship, I began to build the church of God. My mother church in the village had its foundation laid in 1986. Most people that are offspring of that church abandoned the project to old and poor people in the village to build the house of God.

I took over the building project. I did not think of buying a car or building a house though the money will be able to do all that. I channelled most of the money to the completion of the church building. You got to see the beauty of that church! I also bought generator for the church, wired the house and equip the church library to help the pastors to read more. Most of my income were channelled into the church project for complete a year. I bought nothing for myself except the spiritual Christian books that I purchased and my family up keep. I did not think of banking the money and live like others, I remembered the God of my childhood, the God that has been protecting me. Today I can say that I am blessed. Generational anointing of blessings is working upon my life. Today I can say with confidence that I am an international figure. Time will fail me to tell you about the spiritual blessing that follows in terms of spiritual anointing and power that the Lord gave to me, at least I do lay my hand upon mad and insane people and they recover, I speak to people's life and they see results.

> **God is faithful; he is not unrighteous to forget our labour of love.**

God is faithful; he is not unrighteous to forget our labour of love. Praise God!

Woman with alabaster box

There came unto him a woman having an alabaster box of very precious ointment, and poured it on his head, as he sat at meat. But when his disciples saw it, they had indignation, saying, to what purpose is this waste? For this ointment might have been sold for much, and given to the poor. When Jesus understood it, he said unto them, why trouble ye the woman? For she hath wrought a good work upon me. For ye have the poor always with you; but me ye have not always. For in that she hath poured this ointment on my body, she did it for my burial. Verily I say unto you, Wheresoever this gospel shall be preached in the whole world, there shall also this, that this woman hath done, be told for a memorial of her.

-Mathew 26:7-13

> **When you see the act of love you will know.**

See what this woman did? She may not know the implication of her sacrifice. People that give to God sacrificially are those that love God. When you see the act of love you will know. This woman brought an alabaster box containing precious and costly ointment and poured it on the body of Jesus while He sat at meat.

It is so unfortunate that the disciples still at this time were yet to understand spiritual things; they labelled the action of the woman wasteful. The woman who was not always with Jesus understood spiritual thing than the disciples, this woman was actually a sinner but he received salvation thereafter.

Do you know that this Christian race is not all about tittles? It is all about the love that you have for God and it is all about the revelation of God that He has laid in your spirit.

Your sacrifice can lead you to salvation as in the case of this woman with Alabaster box

Jesus admitted that the sacrifice of this woman was born out of the love that she had for him. Let us consider the account of this woman in the book of Luke;

And, behold, a woman in the city, which was a sinner, when she knew that Jesus sat at meat in the Pharisee's house, brought an alabaster box of ointment, And stood at his feet behind him weeping, and began to wash his feet with tears, and did wipe them with the hairs of her head, and kissed his feet, and anointed them with the ointment. Now when the Pharisee which had bidden him saw it, he spake within himself, saying, This man, if he were a prophet, would have known who and what manner of woman this is that toucheth him: for she is a sinner. And Jesus answering said unto him, Simon, I have somewhat to say unto thee. And he saith, Master, say on. There was a certain creditor which had two debtors: the one owed five hundred pence, and the other fifty. And when they had nothing to pay, he frankly forgave them both. Tell me therefore, which of them will love him most? Simon answered and said, I suppose that he, to whom he forgave most. And he said unto him, Thou hast rightly judged. And he turned to the woman, and said unto Simon, Seest thou this woman? I entered into thine house, thou gavest me no water for my feet: but she hath washed my feet with tears, and wiped them with the hairs of her head. Thou gavest me no kiss: but this woman since the time I came in hath not ceased to kiss my feet. My head with oil thou didst not anoint: but this woman hath anointed my feet with ointment. Wherefore I say unto thee, Her

> Giving to the poor is good but that cannot be called sacrifice to God

sins, which are many, are forgiven; for she loved much: but to whom little is forgiven, the same loveth little.

And he said unto her, Thy sins are forgiven. And they that sat at meat with him began to say within themselves, Who is this that forgiveth sins also? And he said to the woman, Thy faith hath saved thee; go in peace.

-Luke 7:37-50

> They are certain thing that comes out of our mouth that appear holy but they are not

You can see that the disciples seriously criticized the action of this woman; they

315

preferred the oil be sold and given to the poor.

If you want fame do the unimaginable

There are certain things that come out of our mouth that appears holy but they are not. There are certain things that we do as good deed but there are not what God want.

Do not be led by sentiment be led by the word of God. Some of you take the things that are meant for the kingdom to the wrong place because the devil has deceived you. It cannot be considered as sacrifice until it is channelled into the right place. Giving to the poor is good but that cannot be called sacrifice to God, it is simply a giving. What you need to do to change your life is not only giving to the poor but also sacrificing unto God.

Jesus declared the woman free from her sin and she left peaceful. Your sacrifice can bring deliverance and peace to you. Sacrifice has made this woman famous; Jesus said anywhere the gospel is preached her name will be mentioned. If you want fame do the unimaginable. This woman did what both the Pharisee and the disciple of Jesus cannot imagine.

Do you know the significance of the sacrifice of this woman? It was Jewish custom to anoint their dead before burial. Jesus is not going to have that opportunity because of the circumstances that surrounds His death that is why the woman brought that oil to anoint His body, not knowing the implication; "*For in that she hath poured this ointment on my body, she did it for my burial.*" That act demonstrates that it is the living that needs anointing not the dead as practiced among the Jews.

Understand also that there was a divine supply here. When God needs a thing to be done for His service He motivates people to do it without them being aware or fully aware of the implications. However, the blessing still follows them because God choose them for that assignment.

I cannot make an exhaustive list of the power of sacrifice; Sacrifice gives one access to salvation, blessing and power.

Sacrifice of God

I have written about the sacrifice of God earlier in this book while I was writing about the sacrifice of Abraham.

God so love the world that he gave his only Begotten Son. Wherever there is love they will be giving. God loved and he gave. They can be no desire for sacrifice if love for God is not in place. The love of God is the motivator of sacrificial giving and when you love God he will love you back. Power is a by-product of God's love.

For God so loved the world, that he gave his only begotten Son, that whosoever believeth in him should not perish, but have everlasting life.

-John 3:16

The sacrifice of God is for the redemption of your life from sin. If you believe in His son Jesus you cannot

> **If you are born of the Spirit you will be like the wind to the kingdom of darkness and the devil cannot tell of your movement.**

perish. You will only perish and perish forever if you fail to believe. You will live in abundance if you believe in the sacrifice that God did by sending his son to die for you. Those that believe are born of the Spirit and the devil cannot trace their life.

The wind bloweth where it listeth, and thou hearest the sound thereof, but canst not tell whence it cometh, and whither it goeth: so is every one that is born of the Spirit.

-John 3:8

If you believe Jesus whom God offered sacrificially for our sins and you confessed your sins and ask for the blood of Jesus to wash you from your sins by faith, then you are born again (born of the Holy Spirit).

To be born again is to be born of the Spirit. If you are born of the Spirit you will be like the wind to the kingdom of darkness and the devil cannot tell of your movement. You become invisible to the kingdom of the devil.

Now you can say this prayer if you want to be a partaker of life that is in Christ Jesus;

Father Lord Jesus, I ask you for the forgiveness of my sins, I ask that your blood wash me from my sins and make me your child. I receive your Spirit within me to enable me live above sin, as from today I am yours in Jesus name.

LIVING SACRIFICE

God appreciate all kind of sacrifice but in the new covenant there is this sacrifice that He requires most from you and I;

I beseech you therefore, brethren, by the mercies of God, that ye present your bodies a living sacrifice, holy, acceptable unto God, which is your reasonable service.

-Roman 12:1

Your body is the temple of God and the temple of God must be kept Holy. Keeping your body holy is a reasonable service that you can offer unto the Lord. Do you commit fornication and adultery or living the lifestyle of sin? Then your body is not the temple of God. As from today lost the desire to sin against God and become thirsty for righteousness in Jesus name.

Indeed there are certain things that provoke power, there are certain things that you can do to remain perpetually in command, there are things that you can do that your generation will never lack a man on the throne before God; one of such thing is sacrificial giving.

> **As from today lost the desire to sin against God and become thirsty for righteousness in Jesus name.**

I will end this section by telling you a testimony that I heard from Pastor Enoch Adeboye of the Redeemed Christian Church of God; he said that during the early years of his ministry he desired to see the power of God because he was not really satisfied with

321

the level of the manifestation of the power of God at that time. He said he will like to see the lame walk and miracles taking place, as he was asking God in prayer, he heard God saying, what will you give me for that? He said God told him to give Him his Pajero jeep, the car that he loved so much. So, he decided to give out the jeep and notable signs and wonders started thereafter. Every move of God is born on the platform of sacrifice.

DEVOTION

The presence of God comes before the power of God, which is the anointing. You cannot have the anointing before having His presence. The disciple has to wait in His presence before the Holy Ghost came, which eventually led to the multiplication of the church.

Devotion is one of the costs that you need to pay if you want the power of God. Jesus had constant time set aside for His devotion.

And in the morning, rising up a great while before day, he went out, and departed into a solitary place, and there prayed.

-Mark 1:35

Jesus always rises up early before the breaking of the day to pray and by so doing He lived a peaceable life and the life of command. He speaks into the day before the day breaks cancelling all the devils work meant to take place that very day. Jesus always had his devotion in a solitary place meaning a quite place. If you are in search of power you must learn to depart into a quite place to pray so that your attention will not be divided.

> **Meditation translates you to the realm of the Spirit to commune with God. Ideas are born on the platform of meditation.**

You will see how your life is going to change as you wake up early to pray and as you set aside time for your quite time of prayer. When I was 17, I do wake up every day by 4a.m to pray till 8a.m. my life actually became better, I will see open vision and hear audibly from God. Till today I still enjoy my quite time of prayer with Jesus.

When you have your devotion, read the bible and meditate on it. They are awesome power in meditation. Great power is being delivered to you when you set your mind to meditate on the word of God. Inspiration only comes with meditation. Meditation translates you to the realm of the Spirit to commune with God. Ideas are born on the platform of meditation. You give the Holy Spirit the time to do His work on you when you meditate on the word of God.

You need to keep the word of God in your heart and meditate on them.

Let me teach you how to draw inspiration from meditating on the word of God; for maximum inspiration, you have to keep repeating the word by saying it out meditatively. As you keep on saying it, the Holy Spirit will begin to shed more light on those words and you will be amazed with the dimension of revelation that you are going to have.

This book of the law shall not depart out of thy mouth; but thou shalt meditate therein day and night, that thou mayest observe to do according to all that is written therein: for then thou shalt make thy way prosperous, and then thou shalt have good success.

-Joshua 1:8

The word; *meditate* actually means 'to mutter', that is, to say it out to yourself.

Devotion without the word of God is a waste of time and reading the word of God without meditation is unproductive.

WAITING

Waiting is not very easy but necessary; waiting is Painful because the bible said hope deferred makes the heart sick;

Hope deferred maketh the heart sick: but when the desire cometh, it is a tree of life.

-Proverb 13:12.

Sometimes we are enthusiastic to do what God wants us to do but it will be proper to allow Him that want to use us to use us at his own time.

Waiting could be painful yet we need to pay the price. I know that waiting is a price because I have experience what it mean to wait especially when you are blessed with anointing. We need to be patience and wait for the fullness of time. God can try our patience through waiting. Patience is one of the fruit of the Spirit. You will be patience if the Holy Spirit dwells in you.

Therefore thus saith the Lord GOD, Behold, I lay in Zion for a foundation a stone, a tried stone, a precious corner stone, a sure foundation: **he that believeth shall not make haste.**

-Isaiah 28:16. Bolden, mine

Patience is therefore a test of your faith. Patience is not just waiting for the passing of time but what you do while waiting.

It was lack of patience that put Saul in trouble;

And he tarried seven days, according to the set time that Samuel had appointed: but Samuel came not to Gilgal; and the people were scattered from him. And Saul said, Bring hither a burnt offering to me, and peace offerings. And he offered the burnt offering. And it came to pass, that as soon as he had made an end of offering the burnt offering, behold, Samuel came; and Saul went out to meet him, that he might salute him And Samuel said, What hast thou done? And Saul said, Because I saw that the people were scattered from me, and that thou camest not within the days appointed, and that the Philistines gathered themselves together at Michmash; Therefore said I, The Philistines will come down now upon me to Gilgal, and I have not made supplication unto the LORD: I forced myself therefore, and offered a burnt offering. And Samuel said to Saul, Thou hast done foolishly: thou hast not kept the commandment of the LORD thy God, which he commanded thee: for now would the LORD have established thy kingdom upon Israel for ever. But now thy kingdom shall not continue: the LORD hath sought him a man after his own heart, and the LORD hath commanded him to be captain over his people, because thou hast not kept that which the LORD commanded thee.

-1Samuel 13:8-13

I have learned that one should not do what one is not supposed to do.

You will always force yourself each time you try to do anything outside the appointed time or something not meant for you to do. Saul forced himself to offer the burnt offering because it is not meant for him to do it. Impatience will always force one into what one is not suppose to do.

> **When your patience is about to run out the answer is at the corner.**

328

When your patience is about to run out the answer is at the corner. Let me tell you how to wait; when you are becoming too impatience deliberately refused to take action and wait a little longer.

I have noticed that each time you are waiting for someone, the moment you changed your mind and move from the agreed point the person will show up. This is because the point at which you change your mind is the point at which he decides. And that is what happens in the realm of the Spirit. The moment the devil motivate you into discouragement is the very moment the answer was given. Impatience is a blessing sensor that displaces people from their blessings. That was what happened to Saul. He was not patient to wait for Samuel to come perform the sacrifice; He took the responsibility upon himself to do the sacrifice, which he was not supposed to do and that cost him the kingdom.

The price you pay for waiting cannot be compared to the after effect.

Zeal and anxiety causes impatience. Zeal is good and sometimes they might be from God for example; *the lord stirred up the Spirit of Cyrus king of Persia;*

Now in the first year of Cyrus king of Persia, that the word of the LORD by the mouth of Jeremiah might be fulfilled, the LORD stirred up the spirit of Cyrus king of Persia, that he made a proclamation throughout all his kingdom, and put it also in writing, saying,

-Ezra 1:1

But we have to be careful because the devil can lay hand on your zeal and use you against the will of God. When you are beginning to develop zeal contrary to instruction (God's word), know that that zeal is not of God. Any zeal that tends to push you when the Lord say wait then know that such zeal is from the devil. The devil always forces (push) but God guides.

Promises are delivered on the platform of patience

Anxiety can make one to become impatience. I can boldly tell you that anxiety is not of God. Watch against anxiety. Anxiety is a habit that can be controlled by discipline and by the word of God.

For ye have need of patience, that, after ye have done the will of God, ye might receive the promise.

-Hebrew 10:36.

There is a difference between the time the blessing is released and the time is being delivered. Without patience you cannot receive the promise. If the apostles did not wait or tarry at the upper room on the day of Pentecost they would have not received the promise of the father, the Holy Spirit.

Promises are delivered on the platform of patience. God knows the right time for delivery after you might have fulfilled the conditions for the promise.

God told the children of Israel after that He given them the promise of the land of Canaan that He will not drive the inhabitants out for them in one year and he will drive them out little by little until they are multiplied (equipped) to take possession of the Land.

I will not drive them out from before thee in one year; lest the land become desolate and the beast of the field multiply against thee. By little and little I will drive them out from before thee, until thou be increased, and inherit the land.

-Exodus 23:29-30.

It is not when we really get the blessing into our hand that they belong to us. They already belonged to us before we handle

> **God is the God of seasons and time**

it in our hand. That it has not gotten into your hand does not mean that God has not given you. God knows the right time he will want us to handle our blessing or when he wants us to operate in it. He knows when we will mature to take possession of our blessing. God will not give us the blessing that will destroy us just as you will not give your car key to your child no matter how much the child cried for it though the car belong to the child too.

God is the God of seasons and time. He said that He will visit Abraham according to the time of life. Though there is no time in the realm of the Spirit, time is one of the things that make our life on earth beautiful and time functions in God not in man. God can collapse the time and he can advance it. God knows the right time to visit; He is the one that want to use you so allow him to use you in his own time.

Waiting is what makes the journey of life smooth. Waiting is what makes driving smooth else, heavy traffic is the result. There are traffic lights in the journey of life to ensure that we had a smooth journey.

Moses could not wait and that is why he killed an Egyptian. Some that fails in their ministry is not because they were not called but because they cannot wait for the right time.

God may give you something but sometimes; He can delay the delivery till you are matured to take up that power or possession;

I will not drive them out in one year lest the land become desolate and the beast of the field multiply against you'.

There are confusions in the churches today because people are impatient, they want to separate the church and have their own ministry. God do not lead that way; learn to be obedient to authority.

I heard the call of God in about JSS1 at age 12 but I waited. The burden was so strong while in the university but I waited. After I left the university the burden became so intense and burning and the vision became clearer but I still waited. Now I can see that the fullness of time has come that is why I am writing this book. God is the God of orderliness, times and season. You need to pay the price of waiting. Lack of waiting breeds discouragement because when you try to lunch out when it's not yet time they will be no manifestation which could cause discouragement.

CHAPTER SIX

IMPARTATION AND DISCIPLESHIP

The power you have obtained after you might have paid the price needed to be imparted on people. The anointing of Jesus Christ is for the benefit of the church and for threat against the kingdom of darkness. We need to impart the power that we have received to bless the church of God, increase the body of Christ and to threaten the devil.

I want to say most importantly that you will begin to abuse power that has been given to you if you are not sensitive to the leading and the inspiration of the Holy Spirit. And when you begin to abuse the power, you become vulnerable to attacks of the enemy.

I was invited by a group of people one certain time to come and minister the word of God to them but their intentions were different. They have heard from certain of my church members in that city, how witches and wizards submit to the authority that I exhibit in the name of Jesus and they are now calling me to try the power that is in me. In the night I had the revelation upon my bed and the Lord revealed all their secrets. When the day for the meeting came I wanted to go and call fire down but the person that gave me the anointing and power told me not to go and I obeyed. The Holy Spirit gave me the power and the directives of how to use the power have to come from Him alone. You will become vulnerable if you disobey the leadership of the Holy Spirit.

Let us look at the story of Jesus;

And when the tempter came to him, he said, If thou be the Son of God, command that these stones be made bread. But he answered and said, It is written, Man shall not live by bread alone, but by every word that proceedeth out of the mouth of God.

-Mathew 4:3-4.

Do you think that Jesus has no ability to command the stones to become bread? He has the power to give mouth and voice to a stones let alone turning the stone into bread;

And he answered and said unto them, I tell you that, if these should hold their peace, the stones would immediately cry out.

-Luke 19:40.

Jesus will not turn bread into stone because He lives only by the words of God. The command to turn the bread into stone was not from God and satan cannot dictate how His power should be used because he didn't own the power and therefore should not control it. That was what exactly explains my refusal to honour the invitation given to me.

> **Satan cannot dictate how His power should be used because he didn't own the power and therefore should not control it.**

If you are not spiritually mature and if you do not know how to hear from God nor understand the scripture, you will become vulnerable to satanic games.

Now I will like to show you how to impart the power of God. The things I will be mentioning here is not the exhaustive list of how to impart the power of God but some of the ways that have been effectively used in the word of God. Most importantly, I will like you to depend on the Holy Spirit for direction.

Laying on of hands

Laying on of hands is biblical. It runs from the Old Testament to the New Testament or from the old covenant to the new covenant.

And thou shalt cause a bullock to be brought before the tabernacle of the congregation: and Aaron and his sons shall put their hands upon the head of the bullock...... Thou shalt also take one ram; and Aaron and his sons shall put their hands upon the head of the ram..... And thou shalt take the other ram; and Aaron and his sons shall put their hands upon the head of the ram. Then shalt thou kill the ram, and take of his blood, and put it upon the tip of the right ear of Aaron, and upon the tip of the right ear of his sons, and upon the thumb of their right hand, and upon the great toe of their right foot, and sprinkle the blood upon the altar round about.

-Exodus 29:10, 15 &19-20

Here you can see that by laying their hands on the ram, their sins are transferred by faith to the ram. The ram here was a symbol of Jesus Christ. They also receive perfection by faith as they lay their hand on the sacrificial ram. This is an indication that power can be transferred by laying on of hands.

We can also see that the anointing and power that was upon Moses came upon Joshua too when Moses laid his hands upon him.

And Joshua the son of Nun was full of the spirit of wisdom; for Moses had laid his hands upon him: and the children of Israel hearkened unto him, and did as the LORD commanded Moses.

-Deuteronomy 34:9

Laying on of hand was a common thing especially during ordination as an official commissioning or impartation of power;

As they ministered to the Lord, and fasted, the Holy Ghost said, Separate me Barnabas and Saul for the work whereunto I have called them. And when they had fasted and prayed, and laid their hands on them, they sent them away.

-Acts 13:2-3

Laying on of hand was also one of the principal way of imparting the anointing of the Holy Spirit. Many in our days and in the bible received the anointing of the Holy Spirit by laying on of hands.

Then laid they their hands on them, and they received the Holy Ghost.

-Acts 8:17

Note that evil spirit can also be transferred by laying of hands remember that sin was transferred to the sacrificial ram as we read above so make sure that sinful and demonic people do not lay hands on you.

Jesus commanded that we will lay our hands upon the sick and the sick will recover meaning that we can impart the power of healing to the sick by laying on of hands;

They shall take up serpents; and if they drink any deadly thing, it shall not hurt them; they shall lay hands on the sick, and they shall recover.

-Mark 16:18

Power of God can be imparted through laying on of holy hands

Through Holy Material

Holy materials taken from men of God can also deliver power. God had taught me that the anointing of God is not only on people but also on things.

> **The anointing of God is not only on people but also on things.**

There was a time my wife had a Dell laptop that we were using together, one day a dangerous virus attacked the laptop. It was so serious that the laptop cannot even boot let alone attempting to remove the virus. Before the laptop boots the virus attack was already in full operation. I took the laptop to experts but they could not remove the virus. I was angry and I said Lord the anointing of God is not only on people but also on things too. I commanded the virus to go in Jesus name and then attempted to switch on the laptop by faith and behold the laptop responded and the virus disappeared. Praise God!

And God wrought special miracles by the hands of Paul: So that from his body were brought unto the sick

handkerchiefs or aprons, and the diseases departed from them, and the evil spirits went out of them.

-Acts 19:11-12

You have seen that handkerchiefs or aprons taken from Paul heal the sick and drives out evil spirit. Know that when you truly carry fire that fire will also be on the materials around you. Anyone that truly carries fires of anointing has that anointing on all material around him.

Anointing Oil

When Samuel anoints Saul the Spirit of the Lord came upon him;

Then Samuel took a vial of oil, and poured it upon his head, and kissed him, and said, Is it not because the LORD hath anointed thee to be captain over his inheritance? ....And it came to pass, when all that knew him beforetime saw that, behold, he prophesied among the prophets, then the people said one to

343

another, What is this that is come unto the son of Kish?
Is Saul also among the prophets?

-1Samuel 10:1&11

The power of the Holy Spirit can flow through the anointing oil from a man of God.

> It is the anointing of the Lord that turns men into wonders

Saul was only looking for his father's Ass when he decided to visit Samuel. He eventually got something beyond what he was looking for; his kingship was revealed. Something must definitely happen in your life each time you visit a prophet.

It is the anointing of the Lord that turns men into wonders. People were surprised to hear Saul prophesying.

When you have the anointing upon your life you will become a wonder to people. You are meant to be envied and not to be pitied.

344

Anointing is what makes the ordinary man to do extraordinary things. Let me tell you that there is nothing that you cannot do, all what you need is anointing. You need anointing for that business, you need anointing upon your life and children, your certificate and your marriage also need the anointing of the Lord. It is only the anointing of God that can create difference between you and your colleagues.

Power can be imparted through anointing oil.

Is any sick among you? Let him call for the elders of the church; and let them pray over him, anointing him with oil in the name of the Lord:

-James 5:14.

I was in my home town one certain time and I decided to visit the general overseer (G.O) of Holy Ghost and Fire ministries, when I got to his house I met him with another pastor from another Pentecostal denomination who actually came to talk to the G.O about her sister's cancer before I walked in.

345

Immediately I entered, the G.O as usual told me that he will like me to minister in his church the following day being Sunday and I accepted. They then incorporated me into their previous discussion and that they will like me to join them in prayer right there for the sister that is plagued with breast cancer. I then suggested that the sister rather be brought to the church where I will be ministering the following day being Sunday. On that Sunday, I spoke on the topic, the Power of a Prophet.

After my message I made the first alter call for those that will like to give their life to Jesus and the second alter call for those that have one form of addiction or the other. As I was about to get away from the pulpit, the Holy Spirit reminded me to pray for those that are sick. At this time, I have forgotten that I told them to bring someone that was sick of breast cancer. I them made the third alter call for the sick and all of them came out.

The Holy Spirit told me to get anointing oil and call all the elders of the church to surround the people. I sprinkled the anointing oil, as they were too many that I cannot lay hands one on one.

After the prayer, I asked those that have immediately received their healing to come and testify. One of the women that

> **There is power in administering the anointing oil.**

testified of her healing was this sister that had breast cancer, she came to testify how she was immediately healed and all the pain and lump disappeared. I asked some women including the wife of the G.O to inspect the breast and they all confirm the healing. The G.O who happens to be the community doctor also confirms the healing of that breast cancer. Praise God!

There is power when we follow the Instructions in the word of God in its simplicity. There is power in administering the anointing oil.

Moses Staff

But lift thou up thy rod, and stretch out thine hand over the sea, and divide it: and the children of Israel shall go on dry ground through the midst of the sea.

-Exodus 14:16

Moses divided the red sea with the rod. The rod that we have today is a prophetic rod of the word of God that can also divide like the rod of Moses. The word is quick and not limited by time and space and can also pierce the soul and spirit meaning that they are powerful not only in the physical but also in the realm of the spirit and can also reveal the thought and secrets in the heart of men bringing them under the anointing and obedience of Christ.

For the word of God is quick, and powerful, and sharper than any two edged sword, piercing even to the dividing asunder of soul and spirit, and of the joints and marrow, and is a discerner of the thoughts and intents of the heart. -Hebrew 4:12

Peter and John's Voice

Then Peter said, Silver and gold have I none; but such as I have give I thee: In the name of Jesus Christ of Nazareth rise up and walk. And he took him by the right hand, and lifted him up: and immediately his feet and ankle bones received strength.

-Acts 3:6-7

The voice of an anointed man can perform wonder, *Pastor W.F Kumuyi was preaching in a crusade sometime ago and there was a mad man moving around on the street that is close to the crusade ground who immediately became healed on hearing the sound of the voice of pastor Kumuyi.*

Our voices are anointed that is why the bible said we should rebuke the devil and He will flee away from us

Submit yourselves therefore to God. Resist the devil, and he will flee from you.

-James 4:7

You can see that it is only the life that has been submitted to God that the devil will fear and flee.

Water

Then went he down, and dipped himself seven times in Jordan, according to the saying of the man of God: and his flesh came again like unto the flesh of a little child, and he was clean.

-2 Kings 5:14

You have to be humble and learn not to disagree with the voice of the men of God. Namaan almost lost his blessing if not by the intervention of his servants. Servants can also have something reasonable to say. Learn to listen irrespective of your status;

But Naaman was worth, and went away, and said, Behold, I thought, He will surely come out to me, and stand, and call on the name of the LORD his God, and strike his hand over the place, and recover the leper. Are not Abana and Pharpar, rivers of Damascus, better

350

than all the waters of Israel? may I not wash in them, and be clean? So he turned and went away in a rage. And his servants came near, and spake unto him, and said, My father, if the prophet had bid thee do some great thing, wouldest thou not have done it? How much rather then, when he saith to thee, Wash, and be clean?

-King 5:11-14

Jesus saliva mixed with mud

When he had thus spoken, he spat on the ground, and made clay of the spittle, and he anointed the eyes of the blind man with the clay, And said unto him, Go, wash in the pool of Siloam, (which is by interpretation, Sent.) He went his way therefore, and washed, and came seeing.

-John 9:6-7

351

The Shadow of Peter

Insomuch that they brought forth the sick into the streets, and laid them on beds and couches, that at the least the shadow of Peter passing by might overshadow some of them. There came also a multitude out of the cities round about unto Jerusalem, bringing sick folks, and them which were vexed with unclean spirits: and they were healed every one.

-Acts 5:15-16

This is the transfer of power by conduction. The power was conducted through the shadow of Peter.

Blood of the sprinkling

The Blood of Jesus is very powerful; the blood of Jesus can speak better things than the blood of Abel. The Blood of Jesus can speak power, redemption and deliverance

And to Jesus the mediator of the new covenant, and to the blood of sprinkling, that speaketh better things than that of Abel.

-Hebrew 12:24

It is necessary that everything be sprinkle with the blood. It is important that you sprinkle your business, your ministry and even your studies and profession with the blood. There is a law of purging that works with the blood and there is nothing the blood of Jesus cannot wash. The blood of Jesus is what washes our sin away.

Moreover he sprinkled with blood both the tabernacle, and all the vessels of the ministry. And almost all things are by the law purged with blood; and without shedding of blood is no remission.

-Hebrew 9:21-22

But where can one get the blood of Jesus? You have access to the blood of Jesus by faith. I sometimes take water and declare it as blood of Jesus, after all even the scientist have proved that blood is about 90% water and

353

since Jesus died as a man his blood must have contain about the same percentage of water too. Water then is a very good representative of the blood. The bible also said that when Jesus prayed the sweat that comes out of his body was as thick as blood (Luke 22:44), that further confirms that Jesus had water in His blood because they will be no sweat without water.

Water and blood was what came out of his side when his side was pierced.

But one of the soldiers with a spear pierced his side, and forthwith came there out blood and water.

-John 19:34

You can take water or anything that contain water and declares it as the blood of Jesus.

God said to Adam anything you call it that it what it will become;

And out of the ground the LORD God formed every beast of the field and every fowl of the air; and brought them unto Adam to see what he would call them: and

354

whatsoever Adam called every living creature, that was the name thereof.

-Genesis 2:19

Note that whatever licence Adam had I also have because Adam means all mankind and we all were in Adam when God gave Adam the power to name things. That is why we have power to name things as human beings. So what I call it is what it is.

I can call that water or liquid (it might be petrol) the blood of Jesus and apply it on my enemy or anywhere I want to.

I once sprinkled the blood of Jesus on my father's compound and all sort of evil and embarrassment that we previously faced seized.

Elisha salt

And the men of the city said unto Elisha, Behold, I pray thee, the situation of this city is pleasant, as my lord seeth: but the water is naught, and the ground barren And he said, Bring me a new cruse, and put salt therein. And they brought it to him. And he went forth unto the spring of the waters, and cast the salt in there, and said, thus saith the LORD, I have healed these waters; there shall not be from thence any more death or barren land. So the waters were healed unto this day, according to the saying of Elisha which he spake.

-2King 2:19-22

Salt and sugar can be applied to your life prophetically for a turn around.

Elisha's stick

And the sons of the prophets said unto Elisha, Behold now, the place where we dwell with thee is too strait for us. Let us go, we pray thee, unto Jordan, and take thence every man a beam, and let us make us a place there, where we may dwell. And he answered, Go ye. And one said, Be content, I pray thee, and go with thy servants. And he answered, I will go. So he went with them. And when they came to Jordan, they cut down wood. But as one was felling a beam, the axe head fell into the water: and he cried, and said, Alas, master! for it was borrowed And the man of God said, Where fell it? And he shewed him the place. And he cut down a stick, and cast it in thither; and the iron did swim. Therefore said he, Take it up to thee. And he put out his hand, and took it.

-2Kings 6:1-7

Ass on which Balaam rode

And the angel of the LORD went further, and stood in a narrow place, where was no way to turn either to the right hand or to the left. And when the ass saw the angel of the LORD, she fell down under Balaam: and Balaam's anger was kindled, and he smote the ass with a staff.

And the LORD opened the mouth of the ass, and she said unto Balaam, What have I done unto thee, that thou hast smitten me these three times? And Balaam said unto the ass, Because thou hast mocked me: I would there were a sword in mine hand, for now would I kill thee. And the ass said unto Balaam, Am not I thine ass, upon which thou hast ridden ever since I was thine unto this day? was I ever wont to do so unto thee? And he said, Nay. Then the LORD opened the eyes of Balaam, and he saw the angel of the LORD standing in the way, and his sword drawn in his hand: and he bowed down his head, and fell flat on his face.

-Numbers 22:26-31

Fear God! He can use anything as power medium to achieve His purpose and that is why we need to be more humble no matter how powerful we might be because it is a privilege He has given us.

Make sure you use the power God has placed in you. Impart it on other people and make disciples for Jesus. We need more anointed people because the work of the kingdom is much and more labourers are needed;

Therefore said he unto them, The harvest truly is great, but the labourers are few: pray ye therefore the Lord of the harvest, that he would send forth labourers into his harvest.

-Luke 10:2

one

DICIPLESHIP

One of the things that made the ministry of Jesus so successful was because He made disciples. Though one of His disciples, Judas Iscariot could not make it, eleven of them made it. When Jesus

> **Discipleship is a vital principle for continuity.**

> **Divine work needs divine support.**

ascended into heaven He sent down His Spirit to continue with His disciple. He had previously instructed them to wait for the Spirit because He knew that the task is such that no human wisdom can carry it. Divine work needs divine support.

It is interesting to know that Jesus taught His disciples, He imparted the disciple with His kind of anointing and that was why He took Peter, James and John to the mount of transfiguration (Mathew 17:1-8).

Discipleship is a vital principle for continuity.

"Go therefore and make disciples of all the nations, baptizing them in the name of the Father and of the Son and of the Holy Spirit, "teaching them to observe all things that I have commanded you; and lo, I am with you always, even to the end of the age." Amen.

-Mathew28: 19-20

> **Jesus did not instruct us to make membership, but rather discipleship.**

Discipleship helps in the transfer of power. Jesus makes disciples and that is what makes the gospel to spread. Jesus succeeded by making disciples and when He wants to ascend to heaven, He instructed us to also make disciples.

The church growth will be affected if we make members instead of disciples.

Discipleship is different from membership. Jesus did not instruct us to make membership, but rather discipleship. I am not against churches having members but we should not put our attention on membership. I have been to so many churches and what I see is membership and not discipleship. In most of those churches that I have been to it is only the Pastors that have anointing not even all the pastors though. Members are as carnal as people that have never heard of Christ. In such scenario we make membership and not discipleship. *In membership the attention is on the church and the leadership of the church but in discipleship the attention is on the kingdom of God and on Christ.*

> **Making disciples implies teaching the followers the life of Christ and how they can also live the life of Christ and teach others.**

Making disciples implies teaching the followers the life of Christ and how they can also live the life of Christ and teach others. Leaders should teach the people how they gain access to the power of God. Any true man of God will talk of his secret and pray for his disciple to be greater than him.

There is transfer of power in discipleship which leads to church growth.

For I long to see you, that I may impart unto you some spiritual gift, to the end ye may be established;

-Roman 1:11

Impartation of spiritual gift leads to spiritual establishment. Contact is necessary for impartation. Disciples should learn to walk close to their masters just like Jesus and His disciples. You go close to your master to be imparted and not to find faults.

There is impartation when we walk closely with men of God. Some years back I was reading my Physics text in preparation for an entrance exam to the university and I heard a voice telling me to go to Bible Standard Church which is under the leadership of Rev. Dr. Ekwo in Akwa Ibom State of Nigeria. As I went to that church the pastor, prophesied that God will want to use me there and I began to fellowship with them.

After some time I began to follow him as he goes about the localities laying hand on the sick and casting out demons with signs following. I helped in guiding those that are falling under anointing. One day, I felt an inner voice within me to also lay my hand on some of the crowd, as I lay my hands they began to fall under anointing. Some fell by mere raising up of my hands.

The anointing of this man of God was imparted on me as I worked with him. Impartation of anointing is real and until we engage in it effectively the Church is not going to grow.

> **Do not be jealous when your mentee and sons seems to outshine you in ministry..... Every child should be an improvement of his father.**

Do not be jealous when your mentee and sons seems to outshine you in ministry. Their success is your success they are your offshoot they are your granddaughters and grandsons and they are your legacy in the kingdom of God through your gospel. Every child should be an improvement of his father.

Elisha's syndrome

So it was, as they were burying a man, that suddenly they spied a band of raiders; and they put the man in the tomb of Elisha; and when the man was let down and touched the bones of Elisha, he revived and stood on his feet.

-2 Kings 13:21

Can you recall that Elijah transfer his anointing to Elisha? And did you know that Jesus send his Spirit to the disciples? But Elisha carried his anointing to the grave. When a dead man was thrown into the tomb of Elisha, the dead came back to life and stood on his feet as soon as his body touches the bone of Elisha.

Anointing is not to be buried, there are meant to be used to bless humanity. Jesus is not always happy with those that bury anointing neither is He happy with those that hide their talents.

Anointing (power) and talents or skills multiply and developed when they are being used. You may not know how powerful you are until you put your anointing and talents to work, that is why Paul told Timothy to stir up the Spirit that was in him;

Therefore I remind you to stir up the gift of God which is in you through the laying on of my hands.

-2 Timothy 1:6.

> **You may not know how powerful you are until you put your anointing and talents to work**

Sometimes you need to be reminded of who you are in Christ or probably remind yourself. You need to be reminded of what you have received by impartation so that you can activate it into action. You are not the same since you were prayed for the other day; you are not the person you use to be right from the day that divine oil touched your head. Your situation have experienced a

366

turn around right from the day you received that word of prophecy even though it seems there was no physical manifestation. All you need to do is to reactivate your faith for delivery. Claim your blessing and begin to do what you cannot do before. Put your mouth to positive confession and your talent and anointing to work by telling the Holy Spirit to re-fire you. It is then you will know that you have really received something of the Lord.

Paul assured Timothy that he had received something by the laying on of hands. He reminded Timothy that all he needs to do is to stir up that anointing, the Greek word that is being interpreted stir means *rekindling with fire*. Sometime you need to call on the Holy Spirit to rekindle your blessing and anointing. Anointing and talents are to be activated into action and not to be buried.

Then he which had received the one talent came and said, Lord, I knew thee that thou art an hard man, reaping where thou hast not sown, and gathering where thou hast not strawed: And I was afraid, and went and hid thy talent in the earth: lo, there thou hast that is thine. But his lord answered and said to him, 'You wicked and lazy servant, you knew that I reap where I have not sown, and gather where I have not scattered seed. So you ought to have deposited my money with the bankers, and at my coming I would have received back my own with interest. Therefore take the talent from him, and give it to him who has ten talents. For to everyone who has, more will be given, and he will have abundance; but from him who does not have, even what he has will be taken away. And cast the unprofitable servant into the outer darkness. There will be weeping and gnashing of teeth.'

-Mathew 25:24-30

If you don't use what you have God will not give more to you. Those that accuse God and felt that minister of God makes money out of people and looks at them as corrupt and fake never succeed, they remain in perpetual darkness.

This man that received the one talent accused Jesus of reaping where He did not sow and gathering where He did not scatter. He accused Jesus of corruption and called Him a thief. Is this not what you say about churches and ministers of the gospel? Is this not the kind of things you say because you did not believe in tithe and offering? *Today you are delivered from that darkness of ignorance that the devil has kept you in Jesus name.*

Make sure you do not bury your anointing; use it and impart the life of others to the Glory of God.

PROPHETIC DECLARATION

These prophetic declarations are divinely package and delivered to me from heaven. They are directed to specific people and God told me that when those people read it they would know.

These declarations are not to be taken lightly, there to be declared in faith and repeated as many times as possible.

I can see disappointments turning to appointments, I can see miracle marriages and reconciliation of broken homes, I can see cancer melting away, I can see a supernatural turnaround, I can see divine intervention in a court case in South Africa, I can see land reconciliation in America, I can see deliverance from suicidal spirit, I can see depression and addiction destroyed, I can see the spirit of fornication arrested, I can see young men and women receiving anointing for exploit through the reading of this book, I can also see divine supply for widows and children and I can see your church growth in Jesus name.

And the LORD said unto Abram, after that Lot was separated from him, Lift up now thine eyes, and look from the place where thou art northward, and southward, and eastward, and westward: For all the land which thou seest, to thee will I give it, and to thy seed for ever.

-Genesis 13:14-15

Moreover the word of the LORD came unto me, saying, Jeremiah, what seest thou? And I said, I see a rod of an almond tree. Then said the LORD unto me, Thou hast well seen: for I will hasten my word to perform it.

- Jeremiah 1:11-12

If you can see what I saw it then means you have seen well and those declarations must come to pass in your life. Remember that these declarations are spirit and the moment you believed them in faith that spirit will jump from the word and will begin to follow you about, working miracles for you.

It is the spirit (Pneuma, breath of life) that quickeneth (Zoopoioun: vivifying, make interesting, appealing, to make live) the flesh profited nothing: the words (rEmata: declarations) that I speak unto you, there are spirit, and they are life (Zoe: life through Christ, everlasting life)

        -John 6:63. *In brackets mine from Greek translation*

Today mark the end of all afflictions in your life in the name of Jesus

You destiny that has been tired to the tree and stagnated is loosed now and henceforth you will begin to experience a turnaround in Jesus name

It is written there is no power but of God, any power that seems to have been ruling your life until now is brought under the anger of God in Jesus name.

This week as the day breaks you will get married in Jesus name.

As soon as you finish reading and practising this book your job will manifest in Jesus name

God is going to do for you what no man can do and you will know that it was the hand of God and you will serve Him more in Jesus name

I command your crippling business to begin to experience a boom in Jesus name

That yoke of intense pain in your body in the form of sickness and diseases are broken in Jesus name

They is going to be a change of law and leadership in your office and in your country that will favour you in the name of Jesus

As from this moment, I command the fire of God to burn on your tongue to speak words of destruction to every form of affliction and embarrassment in Jesus name.

And they rose early in the morning, and went forth into the wilderness of Tekoa: and as they went forth, Jehoshaphat stood and said, Hear me, O Judah, and ye inhabitants of Jerusalem; Believe in the LORD your God, so shall ye be established; believe his prophets, so shall ye prosper. -2Chronicles 20:20

Important Information

For your testimonies, testimonies offerings, love seed, prophet's seed, sacrificial seed, first fruits and all enquiries; write to: zenithoftruth@gmail.com and we will get back to you.